PEMBROK
WIZARDS AND WITCHES

Brian John

Greencroft Books
Trefelin, Cilgwyn, Newport
Pembs SA42 0QN

Printed in Wales
2001

An old woodcut of a woman encountering a trio of skilled magical flyers --a witch, a devil and a wizard. Note that they fly on their besoms with the twigs behind them, unlike the witches portrayed on page 27. The magician, in particular, appears to be very happy in his work.

Chapter One--
Introduction

The Survival of Folk Magic

This is a book about the role of magic in the folk traditions of Pembroke-shire. By "magic" we do not mean, in the modern understanding of the word, "trickery" or "the art of illusion" or even "slight of hand". We mean instead the use of skills or knowledge beyond the comprehension of ordinary people and indeed often beyond the understanding of well-educated scientists and clergymen. In the Old Testament the prophets Moses, Elijah and Joshua were men of God, but they were also magicians, and their status was at least partly dependent upon their ability to "out-perform" the magicians

Moses and the burning bush -- magic trick or Act of God?

and priests who worked for other Gods! Whether we refer to their famous theatrical performances as miracles, magic tricks or Acts of God does not really matter.

The miracles performed by Jesus Christ were also "magical performances" which greatly impressed observers. Both Christ and the old prophets were able to demonstrate a mastery of the physical and mental worlds that was beyond the ken of both their supporters and their opponents. This mastery was also inherited by some of the Apostles and later Christian saints.

At the outset we should distinguish between the main groups of people in Pembrokeshire who had special powers. These were:

1. The wizards or "wise men" who were held to be very learned in the magical arts, having studied human behaviour, medicine, astrology, herbalism and other esoteric subjects. They were supposed to have special powers which enabled them to communicate directly with the supernatural world and to use their knowledge for the good of mankind. They could cure diseases, see into the future, and lift curses through the great strength of their own magic.

2. Black witches (both men and women) who had special gifts but who had allowed greed or ambition to divert them from the true path into evil ways involving curses and spells. They were held to be mean-spirited and vengeful, and were quick to take umbrage. They traded on the fear which they could instill into the minds and hearts of gullible people.

3. The white witches who were less powerful than the magicians or wizards but who nevertheless used their special powers to do good. They made love potions, lifted curses and spells, and could see into the future. They used strange rituals and incantations and often sold their services to those in trouble.

4. Lesser practitioners of magic who had exceptional abilities to see into the future, or to exorcise evil spirits, or to heal sick people through the use of charms, or simply to make contact with the spirit world. Others could discover things through divination. Some of these people would be known today as being specially sensitive or intuitive, and they were often driven by a strong instinct to heal sick minds and damaged bodies.

With the exception of the black witches, those who have practiced folk magic down through the centuries in Wales have generally been held in high esteem. They have also been feared to some degree, since those who have had the ability to predict things, see things which are invisible to normal folk, effect miraculous cures in human beings and their animals, and bring criminals and kings to account have often been assumed in the past to have a "direct line" to God or some other deity. So the Old Testament heroes are variously referred to as prophets and priests, but seldom as magicians. But in all the cultures of the world, with recorded history stretching back 4,000 years or more, there is a recognition that those who have supernatural powers (including tribal shamans and witch-doctors) have a grave responsibility placed upon them not to abuse their power, and history is full of examples of men (and women) who have misused their special gifts for self-glorification or sexual gratification, or in pursuit of political power. The classic story of a "fallen magician" is that of Doctor Faustus, who lived in Germany around 1500 and who was said to have sold his soul to the Devil. His history (based more on fantasy than truth) became so well known all over Europe that in the Sixteenth and Seventeenth Centuries a widespread belief developed that almost all magicians had dark and distinctly unhealthy dealings with the supernatural world.

In ancient Welsh mythology it was assumed that those with special powers were simply blessed in some way with heightened intelligence or a highly developed understanding of the natural world. The oldest stories about Pembrokeshire, including those in **The Mabinogion**, are full of magical episodes, and some of the leading characters were clearly looked upon by generations of Welsh people as great heroes (or villains) capable of magical acts. For example, they could turn themselves into animals or change into the forms of other human beings, thereby causing great confusion. There were also witches who were capable of evil, such as those featured in the story of Peredur. Sometimes it is difficult, in these old stories, to work out whether the heroes are gods or mere mortals, and some of them display nobility, wisdom, frailty and foolishness in equal measure. Their adventures are fantastical and amusing, and sometimes frightening. Rhiannon had magical powers, as did Math ap Mathonwy, Gwydion, Bran and Manawyddan. In Welsh the word *hud* is used for the type of magic portrayed in the old stories, implying enchantment, shape-shifting and transformation but not contact with the world of ghosts or spirits.

Following the advent of Christianity the old heroic and nature gods of the Celtic world were displaced, and as the centuries passed the idea became prevalent that the practitioners of magic were somehow opposed to the "one true religion". Heaven and Hell (one good, one bad) began to replace World and Otherworld (one familiar, one mysterious) as locations in the geography of the public mind. Value judgments began to appear, and Christian people were encouraged by their priests to see in themselves and in others the conflicting forces of good and evil. You were conceived in sin, born evil and became good when saved by the blood of Christ. If you were not "saved" or "reborn" it was assumed that you were under the control of the Devil. So the Devil (who might also be called Satan, Lucifer or Beelzebub) began to come into the business of folk magic, and it is especially noticeable that in the later stories of magicians and witches (ie those tales written down in the 1700's and 1800's) goblins, demons, lesser devils and even fairies begin to appear, showing that the supernatural world was now feared and literally demonized by the Church. Witches and wizards began to be seen as perpetrators of evil rather than as doers of good, and the self-appointed guardians of public decency worked hard to ensure that public respect for "magic, wizardry and witchcraft" was gradually replaced by public loathing.

Witches provoking a hailstorm -- scientifically impossible?

Another thing that happened in the Nineteenth Century was the inexorable rise of science, and an increasing respect for rational thought, natural laws and organized systems of belief. Some of the early magicians were also skilled herbalists and astrologers, and they were among the foremost scientists of their time, but mainstream scientists were not that interested in prophecies, the world of spirits and higher planes of consciousness. They were increasingly seeking to understand the observable mechanisms which enabled the natural world to function, and just as they began to question some of the more primitive and fundamentalist beliefs of the Church they also questioned some of the the simple "folk beliefs" of common people in magic and the supernatural world. With typical scientific arrogance, learned gentlemen eventually began to take the line that anything they did not personally understand was scientifically impossible. So they also mounted a serious assault on those blessed with special powers, and sought to portray them as charlatans and tricksters or even as madmen.

It is amazing, in the face of the twin assaults of clerics and scientists on the "world of the unknown", that Nineteenth Century Pembrokeshire people retained any respect at all for wizards, witches and charmers. But the stories about these mysterious people demonstrate that common folk had a real affection for them, and even to this day rural communities continue to throw up individuals who are known to have special abilities -- for example in communicating with animals or in seeing the future. There are plenty of people in present-day Pembrokeshire who have experienced strange phenomena, seen ghosts or been affected by premonitions. On some occasions, encounters with the unknown are distinctly frightening. I have personally come across several families in rural Pembrokeshire who are viewed with more than a little apprehension by their neighbours on the grounds that "it would not be wise to cross them." About fifteen years ago one old man who was known locally to have special powers was greatly upset by a niece who was intent upon taking over his little hovel and twenty rough acres. He had a few quiet words with his billy goat, who then proceeded to see her off the territory in a most aggressive fashion. Needless to say, the old man and his neighbours were greatly amused.......

What Did Wizards Believe?

It is quite possible that the wizards of West Wales inherited some of the skills and occult knowledge of the druids who were of vast importance in Celtic tribal society around the time of the Romans. The druids presided over religious functions, and were therefore priests, but they were also court advisers, judges, healers, teachers and upholders of tribal laws and traditions. They supervised human and animal sacrifices, and sought to appease, placate and curry favour with a host of small gods and several large and powerful ones. They were also mystics and guardians of the supernatural arts. In other traditions they might have been called Zen Masters or Gurus. After the arrival of Christianity some of them (for example St Illtyd) were converted and even became revered as saints. If the magicians of later centuries really were the successors of a druidic cult this would explain not only the high esteem in which they were held by simple folk but also their

An old and fanciful print of a Druid, carrying wand and oak leaves.

remarkable sense of dedication and duty. There are hardly any stories in Pembrokeshire of wizards who became corrupted by their power, and indeed there are only two or three stories, out of several hundred, which involve a wizard "showing off" his skills in order simply to impress others. There was plenty of ritual, but showmanship was generally not a part of the local wizard's code of practice.

The body of beliefs and rituals handed down by the druids to the wizards is difficult to discern since there is very little written material to go on. Indeed, it was an article of faith among druids that all of their practical and esoteric knowledge should be memorized rather than committed to writing, and in order to achieve this they had to go through a twenty-year "apprenticeship". However, clues to their beliefs have been found in burials, artifacts, tokens and ritual objects all over the Celtic world.

Over a thousand years after the departure of the Romans, a number of interested writers tried to make sense of a jumble of written fragments, symbols, hearsay and inherited memories on the subject of druidical core beliefs. From what we can gather, these were more like Oriental or Gnostic beliefs than those associated with the Old or New Testaments. The druids probably believed that there were three circles of being, and they used the wheel to portray this. At the centre was a place called Abred, roughly equated with the Otherworld or Annwn, where there was a constant struggle between evolution and chaos, between light and darkness. This was where Cythraul or nothingness was to be found, and in modern druidic belief it is called the "still point of being and no-being." The old Welsh tale of conflict between Hagfan and Pwyll described in **The Mabinogion** is deeply symbolic in this respect, suggesting the on-going conflict between good and evil in the Otherworld. Those who resided within this circle may have been dead or alive, and they may have passed through various forms including those of fishes, birds and land animals and even inanimate objects. At last, in the quest for enlightenment, it was believed that humans might be lucky enough to pass across a frontier into a middle circle, into a place called Gwynfyd, in which life was manifested as a pure and rejoicing force where good had triumphed over evil. And the last or outermost circle, which had no outer boundary, was called Ceugant or infinity, a place of ultimate brightness inhabited by God alone. Most people, according to the druids, existed more or less on the boundary between Abred and Gwynfyd, and could move from the one to the other as a consequence of the ways in which they ordered their lives.

This was and is a very subtle theology involving gradations and flows, shadows and twilight, movements towards and away from enlightenment. There are obvious parallels with the traditional beliefs of some eastern religions, and indeed the druids had a strong conviction that the soul was immortal, returning after death to inhabit another body. They taught that death was not to be feared, and saw human sacrifice as a process of "giving" to the gods. They also worshipped a whole pantheon of nature gods and "place gods", some of whom were very specific to small tribal groups or clans.

In the early days of Celtic Christianity the druids had no problem with Christian teaching, because they shared a belief in a benign God who inhabited a paradise to which all could aspire. After about 400 AD many druids became Christians, and the early Church in Wales adopted some druidic beliefs. But then Christian theology developed along rather harsh lines until it became a theology based upon absolutes; you were either saved or damned, you walked either in light or in darkness, your journey through life was either rewarded in Heaven or punished in Hell.

By the 1400's there were only a few vestiges of the old druidic beliefs left in Wales, and the Welsh bards were more interested in storytelling than in philosophy or religion. However, an interest in folk magic was kept alive by a few individuals with special powers, and some of them were students of the occult. They scoured the ancient writings from all over the known world, and synthesized and adapted old systems of belief and ritual to create "guidance manuals" for wizards, apothecaries, astrologers and healers. Inevitably, some of this material found its way into Pembrokeshire from the four corners of Europe and even, in the Age of Discovery, from Egypt, India and the Far East.

Some of the most influential events in the history of magic took place in Germany at the beginning of the Sixteenth Century. There two charismatic individuals called Cornelius Agrippa and Paracelsus brought magic to the notice of the public, and caused great controversy. They both had special powers, and although they regarded themselves primarily as philosophers and students of the natural world they also made a great study of the supernatural. Their interest in the occult was hard for more "material" scientists to accept. Most of their peers were jealous of

their intelligence and mental agility, but it appears that both of them were politically naive, arrogant and even vainglorious, and this did the cause of magic no good at all.

Later on Sir Isaac Newton was a bit of a wizard on the quiet, and among the other famous wizards we can name Anton Mesmer (who gave his name to the verb "to mesmerize") and Jacques Casanova (who was at least as well known in his own time for faith healing and predictions as he was for his bedroom exploits). Nostradamus and Rasputin were also wizards, as were the Count of Saint -Germain, Eliphas Levi, Count Alessandrio di Cagliostro, McGregor Mathers, Madame Blavatsky, and Georgei Gurdjieff. The writers WB Yeats and Bram Stoker were students of the magical arts, although it is not certain that they actually had any special powers themselves.

Nostradamus, a famous Sixteenth-Century wizard and prophet.

Over the last five hundred years or so wizards, both famous and infamous, have been obsessed with a strange and mystical system of knowledge called the Cabala or Kabbalah. This system is reputed to go back to the dawn of history, and its core beliefs are contained in two ancient works, namely **The Book of Creation** (Sefer Yetsirah) and **The Book of Splendour** (Zohar).

The former was written in Hebrew in the 2nd Century AD and the latter in the late 13th Century. The purpose of the Cabala is to show fallen man how to find his way back to paradise, and Cabalists have always believed that if man can find out how to escape from the tangle of ropes and knots that he has created around himself, then he can climb to the highest state of all -- one of total freedom. This blissful state, involving union with God (Kether) can only be reached after clambering through nine states of consciousness including wisdom, beauty, power, love, endurance and majesty. These nine states are known collectively as the Sefiroth, and they are explored or passed through either on the astral plane, or in a trance-like state, or through prolonged study.

Many wizards have devoted themselves to the study of the Cabala and to the practice of rituals associated with it, and to modern minds it may appear as sensible a system of belief as any other. However, the essential emphasis on virtuous living in the pursuit of ultimate union with God was forgotten about by some later wizards, and the careers of such men as Nostradamus, Casanova and Rasputin had more to do with earthly power than with spiritual enlightenment. Some wizards became dangerously preoccupied with the idea of total freedom, and felt that this included freedom from responsibility. People like Aleister Crowley became so preoccupied with total personal freedom that they used other people in a quite ruthless way while living self-obsessed lives involving "sex magic", drugs, occult rituals and satanism. He and others preached the central message "Do what you will", thus distorting the central message of the Cabala, which was much more concerned with virtues including compassion, consideration and self-discipline.

Sadly, because of the intolerance of the Christian Church in the Sixteenth and Seventeenth Centuries the Cabala was driven underground. Wizards and witches literally went in fear of their lives. Underground movements were (and still are) dangerous, both for those involved down below and those left on the surface. One feature of the Cabala was the use of strange geometrical symbols, ciphers and codes, and this had the effect over the years of making the world of magic inaccessible to ordinary folk and creating an aura of secrecy around its practitioners. So occultism and magic moved out of the public domain and into a domain inhabited secretly by wizards and sorcerers who had to be initiated through grotesque rituals into a knowledge of "The Ancient

Wisdom". It was then but a short step into the murky world of secret societies, cults, inflated egos, necromancy, freemasonry and satanism. Magic began to turn into "black magic". Societies like The Golden Dawn (in which Mathers and Yeats were leading lights) started off with noble intentions, but sadly many of their leading figures became besotted with power, not just over themselves but over the natural world and all its creatures. Famous books like **Dogma and Ritual of High Magic, The Secret Doctrine, The Book of Enoch** and **The Key of Solomon** were not really intended to be subversive or seductive, but they became cult textbooks, reviled by the scientific and religious establishment but revered by both good wizards and wicked charlatans.

The Old Gentleman and his Helpers

It is a fact that since the death of Aleister Crowley in 1947 magic has been generally associated with evil, satanism, and even Devil-worship. Crowley was personally responsible for this shift in public perception, since he enjoyed being referred to as "the wickedest man in the world" and as "The Beast." Films and horror stories have developed the theme of magic and evil in recent decades, so that the "cult of the Devil" now appears to fascinate millions of impressionable people. Perhaps the horrors of Twentieth Century warfare also reinforced the idea that there is some elemental force of Evil stalking Planet Earth, and indeed the leaders of many religions have struggled for centuries with the dilemma of Good versus Evil. If God is Love and if the ultimate instincts of mankind are towards goodness and cooperation, how is it that the warring parties of 1939-1945 slaughtered millions of innocent people? How could the Holocaust have happened? Surely there must therefore be an anti-Christ, a powerful force of Evil dragging people away from peace and light and encouraging wickedness on an almost incomprehensible scale? By the same token, is it not reasonable to assume that the Satan who tempted Christ still exists, and can be summoned by those who worship him?

One reason for the high status of wizards in Welsh society was that there was little real appreciation of "The Devil" as a powerful, grotesque and gigantic personification of evil. Therefore, even if the Christian Church in Wales tried to discredit wizards by saying that they were "in league with the Devil" this did nothing to strike fear into the hearts of local congregations. Going back to the time of the druids, the Welsh word *Cythraul* (now used to mean "The Devil") simply meant the opposite of the principle of energy, creation and life. It meant nothingness or emptiness or darkness. The druids believed in a conflict between the forces of darkness and the forces of light, and in their minds unhappiness and misery were associated with separ-ation from the infinity and purity in the outer circle of being. Annwn, the Otherworld, was not particularly a place of terror, but a place

An old print of the Devil, wildly playing his demonic music on a violin.

which had simply not been enlightened. So *Cythraul*, as a personification of this different place and this different state of existence, was to be pitied rather than feared. The Devil, in the oldest Welsh tales, is very much like the pagan god Pan. He is a figure of fun rather than a figure of terror. He is a buffoon and an idiot, with little horns on his head, a funny tail, and goat's hooves where his feet should be. Sometimes he is red, and sometimes he is black. He hides in dark corners or prances about trying to frighten people, and indeed sometimes succeeds in this, but he is easily outwitted by intelligent Welsh people, and at the end of most of the old tales about him he is sent packing with his tail between his hairy legs.

The Devil's task was to tempt honest men and women, but having led them astray (for example, into breaking the Sabbath) he would not congratulate them and shower them with gifts, as one might expect, but punish them! Logical and rational patterns of behaviour were not at all expected of him. But he was accorded some respect, and it was thought to be in poor taste to refer to him directly by name as Satan, *Diawl, Diafol or Cythraul*. So he was generally referred to obliquely as *Y Gwr Drwg* (The Bad Man) or *Yr Hen Fachgen* (The Old Boy), or even Old Nick, and the magicians and witches seldom referred to him at all, directly or indirectly. In polite circles he was called The Old Gentleman.

From the foregoing it may be appreciated that Welsh people have never really taken to the idea of Satan, or the Devil, as he is portrayed in the New Testament or in assorted nineteenth and twentieth century horror stories and films. The fearsome and totally evil Prince of Darkness who stalks through space and time, subverting and destroying and sowing the seeds of chaos and terror, owes more to the Book of Revelation, the theology of St Paul and the strange obsessions of Aleister Crowley than to the subtle beliefs of the ancient druids and bards. Out-and-out wickedness, debauchery and wrong-doing, satanism and depravity have always been viewed with suspicion by the people of Wales, who prefer to see things in shades of grey than in black or white. Indeed, excessive virtue is, in the Welsh tradition, just as distasteful as excessive vice, and this is why small communities have always been remarkably tolerant of human frailty!

The Pant-cou Invocation

When the Rev J Ceredig Davies had the opportunity of looking through the contents of Pant-cou, the home of the most famous wizard in Wales, he found no locked "magic book" full of demons, and indeed it was said by the locals that his "library of magic" had been burned after his death. However, the reverend gentleman did find a large number of ancient tomes, some of them written in Hebrew, Latin and Greek, and books dealing with alchemy, astrology, herbal medicine and so forth. Whatever else the wizard was, he was certainly well read and erudite!

And then Ceredig Davies had an extraordinary stroke of luck, for he found something occult that had escaped the flames -- namely a written and detailed "Invocation" which read as follows:

How to Obtain the Familiar of the Genius or Good Spirit and cause him to Appear
After the manner prescribed by Magicians, the exorcist must inform himself of the name of his Good Genius, which he may find in the Rules of the

Travins and Philermus; as also, what Chonactes and Pentacle, or Larina, belongs to every Genius. After this is done, let him compose an earnest prayer unto the said Genius, which he must repeat every morning for seven days before the Invocation...........

When the day is come wherein the Magician would invokate his prayer to Genius he must enter into a private closet, having a little table and silk carpet, and two waxen candles lighted; as also a chrystal stone shaped triangularly about the quantity of an apple, which stone must be fixed upon a frame in the centre of the table; and then proceeding with great devotion to Invocation, he must thrice repeat the former prayer, concluding the same with Pater Noster etc, and a missale de Spiritu Sancto.

Then he must begin to consecrate the candles, carpet, table and chrystal, sprinkling the same with his own blood, and saying: "I do by the power of the holy names Aglaon, Eloi, Eloi Sabbathon,Anapheraton, Jah, Agian, Jah, Jehovah, Immanuel, Archon, Archonton, Sadai, Sadai, Jeovaschah etc, sanctify and consecrate these holy utensils to the performance of this holy work, in the name of the Father, Son and Holy Ghost. Amen." Which done, the Exorcist must say the following prayer with his face towards the East, and kneeling with his back to the consecrated table: "O thou blessed Phanael my angel guardian, vouchsafe to descend with thy holy influence and presence into this spotless chrystal, that I may behold thy glory etc." This prayer being first repeated towards the East, must be afterwards said towards all the four winds thrice.

And next the 70th Psalm repeated out of a Bible that hath been consecrated in like manner as the rest of the utensils, which ceremonies being seriously performed, the Magician must arise from his knees and sit before the chrystal bareheaded with the consecrated Bible in his hand and the waxen candle newly lighted waiting patiently and internally for the coming and appearance of the Genius.....

Now about a quarter of an hour before the spirit come, there will appear a great variety of appiritions within the glass; as first a beaten road or tract, and travellers, men and women marching silently along. Next there will be rivers, wells, mountains, and seas appearing; after that, a shepherd upon a pleasant hill feeding a goodly flock of sheep, and the sun shining brightly at his going down; and lastly, innumerable flows of birds and beasts, monsters and strange appearance, and which will all vanish at the appearance of the Genius.

The Genius will be familiar in the stone at the performance of the Wizard."

What are we to make of such a strange Invocation? We can simply dismiss it as gobbledygook or as a weird concoction of beliefs and rituals from various cultures and cults. But we might as well assume that something like this was subscribed to by most of the wizards operating in Pembrokeshire and other parts of West Wales. Further, when we look at the Invocation in detail it is more notable for its naive charm than for its association with the devil or with the powers of darkness. There is certainly nothing inherently EVIL in it. There is no mention of the Devil or Satan, and nothing which implies a worship of, or respect for, wickedness or wrongdoing. And note that the word "genius" is used here in exactly the same sense as the word "genie" in the story of Aladdin and the Lamp! There is nothing here which should really be looked on as threatening by the Jews, Christians, Buddhists, Hindus or Muslims of today. Indeed, there are hints and nuances from all of these major religions in the Invocation, as well as phrases that might be familiar to Freemasons, modern druids, members of ancient guilds and orders, and even the organizers of great events of state!

And when it comes to the rituals described in the Invocation, are they really any more extreme or strange (or inherently more absurd) than the rituals involved in a Roman Catholic mass, or a Methodist marriage service, or a Baptist baptism, or a prayer meeting organized by evangelical fundamentalists? A look at the acclaimed film **Baraka** will convince even the most hardened rationalist that ritual -- including the consecration of vessels and furnishings and other articles of worship, the veneration of sacred objects and icons, the calling down of higher powers through ritualized words and music, and prayer and meditation -- are all essential parts of the human condition. In the wizard's Invocation the practitioner is required to sprinkle his own blood onto the ritual objects; but is this really more grotesque than a Christian baptism involving the sprinkling of holy water or a Christian communion involving the symbolic eating of Christ's body and the drinking of his blood?

The Knowing Ones

There have been many wise men or sorcerers in Pembrokeshire over the centuries, ranging from Merlin (Myrddin) the Wizard in the Dark Ages to a number of "quack doctors" in the early part of the twentieth century. Sometimes they were called "conjurors", magicians or enchanters because of their ability to perform what appeared to be magic tricks. In other cultures they might be described as sorcerers. Some who were gifted with second sight are better described as diviners or soothsayers, prophets or seers. Indeed, the type of magic practiced by wizards is called *dewin* in Welsh, implying divination as well as sorcery, and contact with the spirit world.

Wizards are not often referred to as such in local folklore. Instead, the Welsh term *dyn hysbys* (literally " knowing man") was and is used in the Welsh-speaking parts of Pembrokeshire, and this gives a good clue to the role of such men in the community. Incidentally, the experts think that the word "druid" meant "thorough knowledge", and this might confirm the idea discussed above that wizards were the real successors of the druids. Local wizards very seldom did mischief, but were used by members of the public at a fairly mundane level for removing curses or spells and for solving problems or curing mysterious ailments. They were assumed to be able to see into the future, but were generally very reluctant to foretell events because such prophecies (which were almost always correct, whether for good or ill) tended to cause great distress to others.

In the reign of Queen Elizabeth I (the time of the famous magician Dr John Dee) it was believed that Welsh people had a special facility for moving in and out of the spirit world and practicing the magical arts. For example, Glendower, in the reign of Henry IV, is made by Shakespeare to say "I can call spirits from the vasty deep." Closer to home, among the best known of the wizards or wise men practicing in Pembrokeshire within the last 250 years were John Jenkin or Ioan Siengcyn of Nevern (around 1790); Abe Biddle of Millin Dingle (around 1800); William Gwyn of Little Newcastle (around 1800); Joseph Harries of Werndew, Dinas (around 1800 -1810); Wil Tiriet of Caerfarchell (around 1840); Levi Salmon of Cilgwyn, Newport (around 1880); and Dr John Harries (the father) and Dr Henry Harries (the son) of Pant-cou in Carmarthenshire, both of whom did much work in Pembrokeshire around 1820 – 1850. The latter two, often referred to as the Doctors Harries of Cwrt-y-Cadno (Pant-cou), were by far the most famous wizards in Wales. Dr Harries Senior died in 1839 and his son around 1866. Another famous wizard who was also a cleric was Rev Edmund Jones, otherwise known as "The Prophet Jones". He was really from Monmouthshire, but he is thought to have visited Pembrokeshire on a number of occasions in the early 1800's. He made no secret of his own special powers, and he was unusual in that he saw no contradiction between his Christianity and his belief in the world of spirits and phantoms, omens and premonitions.

In the old days many of the wizards had a good knowledge of herbal medicine, astrology and chemistry, and perhaps it was inevitable that in the superstitious mind of the Fifteenth and Sixteenth Centuries they should be accused of witchcraft and even of working on behalf of the Devil. It was put about by many clergymen (who saw wizards as their rivals) that they practiced "the Black Art", and that they used the Devil in the form of various familiar spirits for doing their work. Bulls, donkeys, black dogs, geese, cats, black calves and many other animals appear in the old stories as doing the bidding of various wizards. Sometimes the spirits would be in the form of balls of fire, or stones, or tables or chairs, or even wooden bowls. It was important that these "familiars" or spirits should be summoned in the correct way and dismissed in the correct way, or great harm could come to the magical practitioner. The old story of the Sorcerer's Apprentice shows just how easy it is for things to go wrong, and indeed there are similar Welsh stories of wizards' assistants dabbling in magic with terrible (and sometimes amusing) consequences until rescued by their masters.

People believed that many of the important instructions for dealing with evil spirits were contained in ancient books which were normally kept under lock and key. It was said that old Dr John Harries of Pant-cou took his great book out for consultation only once a year, and that he only unlocked it when on the inside of a magic circle. And according to legend this annual event would always cause a great thunderstorm in the vicinity of Pant-cou. Naturally enough, whenever a violent thunderstorm occurred, the locals would say "Ah, the Doctor is looking in his book today!" And indeed he probably was, for only fools go wandering about outside when the rain is deluging down and the lightning is striking the treetops.

There is one further point relating to wizard's ritual which is worth mentioning here. We have already looked at the links between the beliefs of the ancient druids and the beliefs of the wizards of the Middle

Merlin the Wizard, as imagined by a Nineteenth Century illustrator.

Ages and later centuries. According to the old beliefs of three concentric realms, darkness or chaos is in the innermost circle (Abred) while most advanced mortals inhabit the middle realm of Gwynfyd. We all know that if a wizard wishes to discover the roots of wickedness, or to solve a crime, he needs to stand inside a magic circle. In other words, he must leave the workaday world, cross back into Abred and make contact with the spirits and demons who inhabit Cythraul and who see and understand evil in all its forms. The symbolism of the wizard drawing a magic circle around himself, and then materializing demons and spirits in the course of his ritual is obvious and striking. Having interrogated them and having experienced many terrors, he dismisses them and returns to the ordinary world by stepping out of the circle.

There are very few descriptions in the literature of the fantastical costumes which certain wizards wore when involved in serious ritual. One wizard is described as wearing a long black cloak embroidered with zodiac and cabalistic signs. On his head he wore a tall pointed sheepskin hat with feathers around the brim and crown, with a sheep's tail hanging down from the back. He carried a whip with a small skull fixed to one end and a thong at the other. The thong was made of a long strip of eel skin. Other descriptions indicate that wizards carried and used the chalice, the lamp and the rod or wand. This would be made of almond or hazel cut with a golden sickle in the light of the early dawn and bound with rings of copper and zinc. It had to be blessed or consecrated by another wizard. Sacred oils (mostly made with myrrh, cinnamon, galingale and olive) would be carried and used. Vestments for special occasions had to be made by the wizard himself; he would use purple and gold garments on a Sunday, white and silver on a Monday, and green on other occasions.

Black and White Witches

While most (but not all) magicians or wizards have been men, most of the witches recorded in local history have been women. They have been around for a very long time, and there is evidence that they were active in pre-Christian Celtic society. In the old story of Peredur, the hero encounters nine witches and defeats them. Black witches have traditionally been those who dabbled in black magic and who have been known as capable of doing harm to ordinary folk; some were believed, like Faust, to have "sold their souls to the Devil." White witches, in contrast, were held to be benign, using their rituals and their knowledge of magic to remove curses, heal ailments and help people. They undertook divination, and were assumed to be the inheritors of the wisdom of the druidic priestesses of two thousand years ago.

Both groups of witches created apprehension in the minds of those among whom they lived, and some black witches were actually feared and reviled, but they were not believed to be as powerful as wizards. They were generally people of little or no education, and most of them could not even read. It was therefore assumed that they could not have studied magic or occult matters in depth, and that the local wizard could be counted upon to get the better of them. There are many stories of witches being outwitted or simply "hounded out of town" if they became too troublesome, and if one analyses the Pembrokeshire stories of witches it appears that they were seen as irritants rather than as threats to society. Many of them who were poor and miserable were even pitied, and people seem often to have played little games with them, giving them gifts of food and fuel and clothing in exchange for a promise that they could live free of curses.

This comfortable co-existence of the natural and the supernatural in Wales was in vast contrast to what happened in other parts of the British Isles and mainland Europe. Between 1275 and 1692 it is estimated that over 200,000 women accused of witchcraft in Europe were tortured and put to death, in the most horrible ways. In Germany it may be that the hysteria was created and fed by an infamous book called **Hammer of Witches**, published in 1486, which laid out the rules for the interrogation, torture and execution of witches with maniacal thoroughness. Five hundred years later this book was described in all seriousness as "the book which has caused more suffering than any other work written by human pen."

The German witch-hunts were perpetrated by both the Church and the leaders of various small states. After the Reformation the Protestant states executed fewer witches and ceased their prosecutions much earlier than the Roman Catholic states. In France and Spain the Inquisition specialized in torturing suspects into confessing to the wildest of occult crimes, and many who were appalled at the level of state-sponsored sadism were too terrified to protest.

In Scotland, during the years of the Penal Witchcraft Act (1563 to 1736), around 5,400 people were put to death following convictions for "traffic with the Devil". The evidence against them was generally very scanty indeed, and in the great majority of cases there were no proper trials. Both Protestants and Roman Catholics used accusations of witchcraft as a means of terrorizing their religious opponents.

In England there was a greater degree of tolerance towards those involved in "unnatural behaviour", but nevertheless sadistic individuals like Matthew Hopkins, author of **Discovery of Witches** and the self-styled "Witchfinder General", succeeded in putting to death hundreds of poor people in the name of God between 1644 and 1646. It is uncertain how large the total death-toll was in England during the witch-hunts, but it must have been over 2,000.

In Wales, so far as we know, there is not a single record of a trial resulting in the conviction and execution of a witch. Three witches were executed in Broughton, Flintshire, in 1656, but they were actually convicted in Chester.

An old woodcut showing witches being burnt at the stake during the witch-hunts of the Sixteenth Century. One of the witches, as she dies, is being taken away to Hell by a fiery serpent.

The appalling persecution of so-called witches is now recognized as something that flowed from mass hysteria, and it is also widely recognized that this madness was fuelled by a Roman Catholic Church which was losing public and political support and which needed "diversions". It suited the Church fathers very well to pretend that witches and Devil-worshippers were threatening the very foundations of society and were seeking to lead people away from God. At the peak of the persecution, especially in Germany, anybody who had a grudge against a neighbour, or anybody who coveted another person's possessions, could make an accusation of witchcraft on the flimsiest of pretexts in the reasonable expectation that arrests, interrogations, tortures, confessions and executions would follow. Nobody was safe, and even the smallest deviations from "normal" behaviour were likely to be seized upon and followed by accusations of witchcraft.

The European "witchcraft hysteria" was accompanied by sadism on a vast scale, and there was very often a sexual element. A celibate Roman Catholic clergy was heavily involved in this, and many of the most active "witch hunters" were perverts who obtained sexual gratification from the intimate interrogation and examination of terrified women. The procedures were all laid out in the **Hammer of Witches** and in Hopkins' pamphlet **Discovery of Witches**. Because it was widely assumed that witches routinely had sexual intercourse with the Devil himself, and with lesser demons, there were almost always strong sexual overtones in the questioning of suspects. It was assumed that "imps" or familiar spirits fed from small wounds or "paps" on a witch's body. Denials were disregarded, and sometimes the smallest wart or other mark on the skin of an accused person was sufficient to convince the prosecutors of black magic rituals or devilish sexual practices. There was blatant sexual sadism in the tortures inflicted on poor innocent souls; and every time a so-called witch "confessed" under torture the stereotype was confirmed and the hysteria increased. At the height of the hysteria every birth which involved a deformed baby immediately resulted in the rumour that the child was "devil's progeny", and almost inevitably both mother and baby would be put to death.

So why was it that the people of Wales refused to have anything to do with the terrifying witch-hunts which raged across the rest of Europe? A number of related facts may be cited by way of explanation.

(a) Witches were actually accepted in society in the same way as labourers, coopers, millers, dairymaids and nurses were accepted. In other words, they were seen simply as people with special skills in the realm of divination or magic, just as others had special skills as knitters or wood-carvers. By and large, they provided valuable services through the healing of diseases, selling herbal remedies, providing lucky charms, choosing "auspicious dates" for planting or harvesting, and performing simple rituals. As mentioned above, they were sometimes viewed with suspicion and apprehension, but they were never viewed as personifications of evil and never accused of threatening the stability of Church or State. The enlightened view which led to the repeal of the Witchcraft Act by the UK Parliament in 1951 appears to have prevailed in Wales more than four centuries earlier!

(b) Most witches in Wales were acknowledged as the natural successors of the priestesses and helpers who assisted in the rituals of the pre-Christian religion. They were linked in this way with the druids and the bards, and even after the passage of 1500 years people found it hard to accept that they were in league with the Devil. To a degree they benefitted from the goodwill shown towards wizards, and most people thought that they had access to less powerful magic. Broadly, it was assumed that their purpose in life was to uphold public and private virtue and -- maybe -- to inflict minor punishment on miscreants. True, some witches enjoyed their power, played about in covens, flew around on broomsticks, summoned up "imps", turned themselves into cats and hares when it suited them, and sometimes did mischief, but these personality defects were really no more serious than those demonstrated by their neighbours!

(c) In the Sixteenth and Seventeenth Centuries, when anti-witch hysteria was at its height in other parts of the British Isles, the conflict between Roman Catholics and Protestants in Wales was a fairly low-key business. For example, there was only one Protestant martyr in Pembrokeshire, burned at the stake in 1558. By and large, people adapted very easily to whichever Church was currently in the ascendancy, and by the time that "hard" and intolerant nonconformism gained popularity in the Eighteenth Century the witch-hunting era was long gone.

(d) As mentioned above, Welsh people have never had any great respect for the Devil as "The Prince of Darkness". That idea was, after all, only invented by St Paul and developed by the early Church fathers. Even after the Nonconformist Revivals, with their emotional emphasis on sin and forgiveness, evil and redemption, Heaven and Hell, there was very little respect paid to Satan. The early Baptists and Methodists in Wales may have preached a message that owed more to the Old Testament than the New, but their theology did not alter the old Welsh view of Satan as a sort of demon (among many other demons) whose job it was simply to help God in the punishment of sin.

(e) Although individuals who believed themselves to have been "hexed" or cursed by witches certainly felt threatened, we cannot assume that whole communities felt threatened. Even at the time when Matthew Hopkins anjd John Stearne were persecuting the people of East Anglia in the 1640's, Pembrokeshire people knew exactly how to deal with witches. Sometimes spells and curses could be removed by negotiation or by outwitting a witch. In more serious cases, the principle generally was to fight bad or harmful magic with even stronger good magic. So a curse or a spell placed by a local black witch would be removed by a stronger spell from a white witch or a wizard. This kept the magic practitioners in gainful employment, and gave small communities plenty to talk about. If witches became too obsessed with extortion or with spells against their neighbours, or if they were too blatantly involved in perversion, they were simply sent packing. There was hardly ever a need to go to court or to involve the law. When somebody who was accused of being a witch was hauled up before the magistrates, cases were normally dismissed, but if the accused felt that she had had a "close shave with the law" the experience was often sufficient to lead to a change of behaviour or a change of address!

Witchcraft Beliefs

While witches were accepted, or at least tolerated, within almost every community in Wales, there nevertheless developed a whole lexicon of "witchcraft lore." Some of the beliefs about witches certainly go back to pre-Christian days, and they are not that different from the beliefs concerning witches in South America, Africa and Asia. In other words, it seems that every society, no matter how primitive or advanced, has maintained, over the millennia, a belief in the supernatural and a conviction that certain individuals can use magic for good or ill. Other beliefs (for example the belief that witches are "in league with the Devil") are much more recent, and can be traced to the Middle Ages. Shakespearean plays including **Macbeth** perpetrated many crude beliefs about witches and witchcraft, and it has been argued that Shakespeare and other populist writers of the time both reflected and contributed to the mass hysteria surrounding the witch hunts of Sixteenth and Seventeenth Century England. Some of the beliefs about witchcraft rituals are pre-Christian, others are perhaps five hundred years old, and yet others owe their origins to recent horror films and novels. Computer games about black magic and about the conflict between good and evil are now adding yet more fanciful items to the "witchcraft lexicon."

So what were witches supposed to believe? Back in the time of the Celtic tribes they may have subscribed to the same core beliefs as the priestesses, attendants and holy virgins who worked with the druids, but they dabbled in the supernatural and may have worshipped the "darker" gods. We can be sure that later witches did not have as comprehensive a set of beliefs as wizards or "knowing men", but some of them certainly knew something about the Cabala and the other magic books, and felt themselves to be the inheritors of the wisdom of the priestesses and druidical handmaidens of pagan times. Some witches knew about an old document called "Aradia" or **The Gospel of the Witches**. This suggests that witchcraft in Europe was originally based in prehistoric fertility cults, involving magic rituals designed to ensure the survival of primitive tribes and to bring hunting success. Later, it evolved into a cult involving the worship of the Roman goddess Diana. Later still, witchcraft was developed by the gypsies and other groups, and was caught up in the social protests of the Middle Ages. Poor people hoped that witchcraft, ancient rituals and pagan beliefs might offer them more than they were offered by a wealthy, corrupt and intolerant Church. The terrors associated with the Inquisition may have cowed thousands of people into submission to the will of the Church, but thousands of others must have been driven to the belief that paganism was preferable; it appeared kinder, gentler and more tolerant of personal imperfections.

Even today, white witches believe that they are keeping alive "Wicca" or the old pagan religion, involving a profound respect for the earth and for all living things. They worship the Great Earth Mother, the oldest of all the ancient gods, and also the Horned God (appropriated by the Christian Church as an image for Satan in its concerted effort to eradicate paganism). They believe that their rituals reflect their respect for nature and ensure the continuing fruitfulness of the earth. Other rituals enhance the prospects for "wish fulfillment" by individuals who are sick or troubled in some way. Healing is at the core of many of the rituals. The belief in the power of the will is not dissimilar to the belief in the power of prayer in the Christian Church, and even outside the Church there is today a widespread belief in the idea of one person or a group of persons "sending positive (or negative) vibes" in the direction of another person or group.

If we go back to the Eighteenth and Nineteenth Centuries it is probably true to say that there were almost as many belief systems as there were witches. Some of them were certainly cynics who deliberately encouraged their neighbours to see them as witches because they enjoyed the notoriety, status or power that this gave them. Others were poor lonely old women whose only crimes were to live alone, to have stiff joints and to wear black clothes. Sometimes the ownership of a black cat or a big black cauldron was sufficient to attract the "witch" label! And once labels were given they tended to stick, making these poor old women more isolated, more hungry and more frightened. Many of them discovered that the easiest way to survive was simply to make the most of being labelled as a witch, by placing curses (or threatening to place curses), conducting strange rituals and otherwise playing the part expected of them, thereby guaranteeing the provision of fuel, cast-off clothes and food as placatory offerings from the people who lived around them.

At the other end of the spectrum there were people who were certainly mentally ill and who suffered from a variety of behavioural problems. Today these sad unfortunate people are helped and even supported, but two hundred years ago they were feared and usually ostracized by society. There is no doubt that some of them were cruel and even sadistic, harming themselves and other innocent folk, performing grotesque rituals (sometimes with a very strong sexual component) and quite genuinely believing themselves to be in league with Satan. There can be no doubt that some of those who were caught up in the British witch-hunts were by no means innocent, and that they were hung or burnt for real crimes and for real harm inflicted on others. Murders (sometimes justi-

An old engraving of witches in full flight. An old hag is teaching a young novice how to fly. It is reputed that the sketch on which this engraving was based was made by the artist Goya.

27

fied as "sacrifices") were really committed by witches and their accomplices. Anybody who reads the old records of the witchcraft trials will recognize that there were some witches who were actually attracted by a life spent in pursuit of evil. Some were masochists or sadists. Some went to the stake believing that they were off to join Lucifer, just as Christian martyrs went to the stake knowing that there was a place for them in Heaven. Obsessions, delusions and fantasies, dreams and visions have always been features of the human condition.

Today there appears to be just as much variety within the world of witchcraft as there ever was. Most witches who subscribe to Wicca are kind, gentle and caring people who would not appear out of place in a Baptist Church vestry. Indeed, they would claim to subscribe to many of the same core beliefs and values as Christians. Their belief system actually owes much to the writings of Margaret Murray (around 1925) and Gerald Gardner (in the 1950's), both of whom believed in the idea of an ancient religion or fertility cult which pre-dated Christianity and which needed to be kept alive. Gardner wrote **Witchcraft Today** and **The Meaning of Witchcraft**, which became handbooks of ritual, and a collaborator named Doreen Valiente promoted the role of the Earth Goddess as a focus of ritual and worship. There are those who argue that Wicca is just as much an "invention" as the latter-day Druidism promoted so enthusiastically by Iolo Morgannwg -- and most would agree that it is essentially harmless.

On the other hand there are distorted witchcraft cults which are obsessed with sexual rituals and which actively practice evil black magic. Satanists practice a sort of perverted Christianity. Some of them use a book called **The Satanic Bible** by Anton La Vey, known variously as "The High Priest of Hell" and "The Black Pope of America." His First Church of Satan was inaugurated on 30 April 1966 (Walpurgis Night and the great feast of the witches' year) and has attracted many psychologically disturbed people and students of the occult. It has its own version of morality which is called "satanic morality". Its preaching of indulgence instead of abstinence, freedom instead of discipline, and its glorification of carnal pleasures has caused outrage in the United States, bearing as it does many echoes of the belief system of Aleister Crowley. Many of the evil cults of America are -- perhaps inevitably -- associated with the use of hallucinogenic drugs and with the drug trade. As in many other cultures there are opportunistic links between religion and crime.

Pembrokeshire Witches

Returning to more innocent times, we can create a stereotype of the typical Pembrokeshire witch of the Eighteenth Century. She normally lived alone in a small cottage. Perhaps she was a widow or an old maid, and perhaps she had been abandoned by her own family. She dressed in black, and she survived by begging or undertaking small services for her neighbours. She cast spells and placed curses if she was a black witch, and removed them if she was a white witch. According to the locals, she had the ability to turn herself at will into either a black cat or a hare, and sometimes into other animal forms as well. She probably belonged to a coven of thirteen, and she and her colleagues met up for strange rituals in woodland glades or on hilltops or in caves, especially on the eight auspicious dates (sabbats) including Samhain (Halloween), Yule and Beltane.

She had the ability, so it was said, to fly through the air on a besom or broomstick. If she was a powerful witch, she could stand within a magic circle and summon demons, ask them questions and make them do her bidding. She could exorcise ghosts and demons from houses, and cast out demons inhabiting the bodies of poor suffering human beings. She could cure animal ailments. She knew a great deal about herbal remedies, and could mix up magic potions. She stirred up strange brews (using hemlock, belladonna, foxglove, vervain and rue) in her big black cauldron. She was on good terms with vipers, billy goats and toads. She could write out or recite magic charms. She could foretell the future, and knew when people were to marry, give birth or die. She could conjure up storms as punishment or bring rain to end a drought. She could see corpse candles and other strange omens. She could expose wrongdoers. She could entrance animals and make machines break down through the force of her magic. And overall, it was best to stay on the right side of her, for if you crossed her you, or your loved ones, or even generations to come, might be forced to suffer the unfortunate consequences..........

Witches could be dealt with in a variety of ways. As indicated above, you could appease them by being a good neighbour, providing them with food and fuel. You could pay them for providing "protection" or for writing out magic charms or for marking your house or your animals with good luck symbols. If you felt that you had been cursed, you could pay to get the curse removed, or pay somebody with stronger magic to do this instead. You could even pay to get a witch to place a curse upon a weaker witch, but this was not thought to be good etiquette. You could remove a witch's power over you by drawing her blood; and there are many stories of people who felt safe once they had managed to scratch a witch on the cheek or on the back of the hand. Alternatively you could achieve the same result by injuring an animal (mostly a hare or a cat) thought to be a witch in disguise. Another way of reducing a witch to impotence was to force her to read out a passage of holy scripture, or to pronounce a Christian blessing, over someone who had been bewitched. Sometimes a special charm might do the trick. Very often trickery or bribery had to be employed in order to get a reluctant witch to cooperate, and there are also many records of brute force being used. Where a witch was not amenable to persuasion, and if she persisted in her wicked ways in spite of the cajoling of clerics and friendly wizards, she would normally be sent packing and her cottage might even be burnt down. As we have seen, even during the time of the witchcraft laws the magistrates were seldom used, and there are very few records of the sadistic "trials by water" and other trials used in Germany and Scotland to decide whether accused women were or were not genuine witches.

A very old woodcut portraying the death by hanging of three witches. Note the strange menagerie of "familiars" including a mole and two monkeys!

There must have been hundreds if not thousands of witches in Pembrokeshire down through the centuries, and until quite recently every self-respecting town, village and hamlet had at least one. Some of them still do have a resident witch. Witchcraft often went in families, with one generation after another demonstrating special powers and dabbling in magic. There are hundreds of stories of witchcraft still in circulation, but for understandable reasons the real names of witches were often suppressed by their families, and white witches were not accorded the same degree of respect as magicians. Most of them did not become local "folk heroes" like Joseph Harries or Abe Biddle. On the other hand some ill-tempered or wicked witches are known by name, and some of them figure prominently in the stories that follow. We can mention Hannah of Walton West (c 1800), Maggie of Pontfaen (c 1820), Old Moll of Redberth (c 1840), Dolly Llewellin (c 1850) of Carew Newton, and Betty Foggy (c 1850) of Pembroke Dock. Stories have survived of two male witches, namely Tom Eynon of Lamphey, who lived around 1840, and Ben Volke of Canaston Bridge, who was a direct contemporary of the wizard Abe Biddle.

Charms and Divination

As mentioned at the beginning of this chapter, Pembrokeshire communities have thrown up very many people over the centuries who have had healing or other skills denied to ordinary folk. Those who are blessed with peculiar abilities do not always feel themselves blessed, and indeed there are many stories of people who have found their talents hard to control or to understand. Embarrassment or puzzlement often goes with special healing skills, and there are stories of healers who try to hide their abilities or who look upon them as impositions or burdens to be carried through life. The expectations of sick folk and their families are often heavy indeed. Other skills include second sight and the ability to foretell events or to see omens and portents such as corpse candles and phantom funerals; but we will not consider these matters here since they deserve treatment in much greater depth. We will restrict ourselves in this book to "folk magic" involving special powers or contact with the supernatural world. However, we should not forget that charms, charming, faith healing, dowsing and divination are claimed by many to require no special skills, and as such they may all come under the heading of "low grade magic." In other words, the belief is that we all have hidden powers which can be "uncovered", developed and used for the good of our neighbours.

 Charms have been used for centuries to bring good luck or to counteract the influence of witches. The basic idea is an ancient one, involving a very simple ritual (for example the writing out of a certain verse or the drawing of a "magic" symbol) and the belief that a token or icon can provide a protective shield around a person or a property. This simple idea was and is used all over the world, in all cultures and religions, in rural and urban communities both primitive and sophisticated. In Christianity the cross is of course the basic "charm" used to ward off evil, but other symbols assumed to provide protection are images of the Virgin Mary, relics including bits of bone, strands of hair and pieces of cloth, and the vessels used in holy communion. There is no particular logic to the use of these charms, and no scientific evidence that they actually work. All that matters is the belief system of the individual and a conviction that the charm itself is authentic and efficacious.

In the local stories about witchcraft Christian charms feature prominently as protection against spells, but there are many other charms which have been used by generation after generation since pre-Christian times. For example, twigs or wands of ash, oak and birch are supposed to reduce the effectiveness of spells, and vervain and rowan are supposed to have extraordinary properties. Hazel was supposed to render witches powerless. Another plant supposed to purify individuals and houses and to remove evil spirits is St John's Wort. Charms involving the word "Abracadabra" and written on special parchment were said to remove hexings and counteract curses, especially if they were placed exactly where instructed by a magician (for example, next to the skin of a bewitched person, in a bottle in a dairy where the milk would not turn to butter, or tied around the neck of a sick horse). Pentacles could be cut into a tree or a door-post to ward off spells and evil spirits. A ball of crystal, or a bowl of salt, or a clean nail could provide protection, as could a circular piece of metal taken from a coffin and then worn over the heart. Stockings worn inside out could provide protection against witches, as could a four leafed clover picked in May and a snake's fang carried close to the skin. A silver coin taken from a church offertory box and melted down and made into a ring was a sure protection against fits. A horse shoe nailed above a door would deter evil spirits, as would a piece of red ribbon fixed to a child's cradle or tied to a cow's tail. Iron generally was thought to counteract the power of the witch, and in some cases a bewitched person was asked to drink water in which a piece of red-hot iron had been cooled.

Those who had special skill in the use of charms were known as "charmers" and they were probably consulted more in the old days than apothecaries and doctors. They tended to specialize, so that one charmer might be known for healing conditions involving bleeding, another might remove warts, and another might cure cancer. Wands and written charms were used by these specialists, but sometimes they used strange invocations and spells handed down within certain families. Some of them used lengths of woollen yarn to "measure" or diagnose an illness. The yarn might be dipped into beer or into a saffron mixture before being tied around a patient's wrist or ankle. Charmers might also use "walking" rituals or certain stylized movements of the hands, and in cases where there was an actual laying-on of hands there may have been an element of faith healing. Christian rituals and blessings were sometimes used, but other charmers seem to have come from a pagan tradition and used the word "abracadabra" and magical symbols.

There is no doubt at all that many charmers and white witches had an excellent knowledge of plant properties and herbal remedies. There is a vast literature on this subject, and just a few examples will suffice to show just how widespread was the belief in the healing properties of plant leaves, extracts, oils and powders. Rosemary boiled up with honey in a jar of ale was known to cure coughs. An ointment containing ragged robin was a cure for snake bites. Club moss was efficacious against diseases of the eye, but only if collected at sundown on the third day of a new moon. Apple juice was potent against warts. Fennel was supposed to strengthen the constitution, and the lady's mantle was said to "restore feminine beauty, however faded, to its early freshness." Angelica was supposed to be a remedy against hydrophobia. Thyme was recommended as a treatment for rheumatism. A potato carried in the pocket was a good charm against rheumatism. The cowslip and the hop were always thought to help in inducing sleep among those who were troubled or in pain. A poultice made from comfrey, cucumber and marigold was used in the healing of burns. Mallow, clove and camomile were said to reduce the pain of toothache. Some charmers knew how to make hundreds of infusions, decoctions and poultices, and when they used them in treatment they would often recite little rhymes and ditties which no doubt increased their effectiveness.

On the matter of divination, many writers have pointed out that real folk magic was involved since no specialist diviner was actually needed. However, there was also a widespread belief that there were dangers involved in playing with supernatural forces, and the literature is full of stories in which "amateur divination" goes wrong with disastrous results. Today we have a similar morbid "fear and fascination" relationship with tarot cards and ouija boards; most of us refuse to have anything to do with them in case anything goes wrong, but others appear unable to resist the excitement involved. Traditionally, therefore, skilled diviners were called upon to help those who were crossed in love, or those who had lost valuable items or who wished to receive answers to some troublesome question.

Diviners used many different techniques, some of which were unique to themselves. In the bad old days, the druids interpreted the death throes, and "read" the entrails, of human sacrificial victims. More recently, diviners might "read" the clouds or the wind, or see answers to questions in the shape of trees or in the behaviour of animals. They might use such items as keys, Bibles, holy crosses made of rowan, healing stones, pieces of cloth, bones, and wisps of hair in their work. They might use candles and pins in romantic divination, and there is a very old belief that a shoulder of mutton should be used in certain ceremonies. Cards were sometimes used for divination in urban areas, and tea-cup divination was widely practiced in Pembrokeshire. Bowls of water were used in some ceremonies, as were items of clothing and bits of straw. Mostly the rituals performed individually or in groups were designed to ascertain the identity of a future husband, or the prospects for child-bearing, or for testing the love of a suitor.

Finally dowsing can be seen as a form of divination, for it involves a search for answers and a strange interaction between the human body and "unknown forces." Skilled dowsers certainly have special skills, but some authorities claim that anybody can dowse for water or discover "earth energies" or ley lines. Traditionally a forked hazel twig is used, but metal coat-hangers, whalebone strips from old corsets or even strips of plastic are adequate substitutes. Pendulums are often used in dowsing, with the answers to questions revealed through the movement of a weight held on a string. Maps are sometimes called upon, and there is incontrovertible evidence of "map dowsers" finding lost items, identifying the spots where crimes have been committed, finding missing persons, and so forth. The strange thing about dowsing is that it seems to work remotely, so that a pendulum held over a map of another region or even another country may identify a grid reference for something which the dowser is inquiring about. When this happens scientists shake their heads and complain that some trickery must be involved.

But in this field, as in all the other fields of magic, the most sophisticated of scientific investigations have failed to provide us with explanations for many strange phenomena. Wizards, witches, charmers and diviners appear to be capable of tapping in to forces as yet inadequately explained, and in looking at the stories about these fascinating people we are reminded forcefully that mankind does not really wish -- even today -- to know everything about everything. Perhaps we need the supernatural to remain just beyond the reach of most of us, and perhaps we all need to maintain some mystery and magic in our lives.

GLOSSARY OF MAGICAL TERMS

Abracadabra: the archetypal "magic word"
Abred: a place of struggle and chaos, equivalent to the Otherworld
Asswynaw: to create or form something by magic
Annwn: Otherworld or underworld
Aradia: the "witches' gospel"
Augury: ritual divination, originally based on the study of bird flight
Awenyddion: poets who speak while in a trance
Bard: an entertainer, poet or musician keeping alive druidic tradition
Beltane: one of the seasonal festivals of Druidry and Wicca (1st May)
Cabala (Kabbalah): a mystical system of knowledge used by wizards
Ceugant: a place of infinite brightness inhabited by God alone
Charm: a symbol used in simple magic for wish fulfillment etc
Cipio: levitation or transport through the air by magic
Codi cythreuliaid: to summon demons of devils by magic
Consurio: to conjure or bewitch
Consurwyr: a magician or man with special or supernatural powers
Coven: a group of witches (normally between 2 and 13)
Curse: a spell or "ill-wishing" directed at an enemy or rival
Curse tablet: a lead or pewter "curse" tablet from druidic times
Cyfaredd: charm, fascination, spell
Cyfarwydd: a prophet or seer, or a skilled teller of stories
Cythraul: nothingness, chaos in druidic belief
Cythraul: devil
Dewin: diviner, magician or sorcerer
Diafol: the Devil
Diana: Greek goddess worshipped in the early days of witchcraft
Diawl: devil

Divination: prophecy or telling the future
Druid: a priest and protector of the old pre-Christian religion
Dyn hysbys: a wise man or wizard (literally : a knowing man)
Familiar: a spirit invoked during magic ceremonies
Filidh: men with special powers including prophecy and divination
Genius: a genie or good spirit invoked by magicians
Green Man: pagan god of fertility and renewal
Gwr Drwg: the Bad Man (oblique reference to the Devil)
Gwraig hysbys: witch
Gwyddon: hag, witch or sorceress
Gwrach: hag, witch
Gwrach y Rhybyn: screaming banshee or spectre
Gwynfyd: in druidic belief, a place where good triumphs over evil
Horned God: pagan god representing power and fecundity
Hud: enchantment, shape-shifting or transformation
Hudol: magician or sorcerer
Imbolc: one of the old Druidic/Wiccan festivals (1st February)
Ju-ju: witchcraft practiced in primitive societies
Kether: God or the ultimate state of bliss believed in by Cabalists
Lledrith: illusion created by magic
Llen hud: magic mantle used to make one invisible
Lughnasadh: a Druidry and Wicca festival (1st August)
Magick: term used by Aleister Crowley for magic involving satanism
Oracle: a shrine or place used for divination or prophecy
Paganism: nature-based pre-Christian religion (including druidism)
Pentacle: a geometric sign used in magic
Prince of Darkness: a modern term for the Devil
Rheibio: to curse or bewitch
Rheibiwr: a male witch
Sabbat (Sabbath): A seasonal festival or meeting of witches
Samhain: an important Druidic/Wiccan festival, equivalent to Halloween
Satan: Lucifer, Beelzebub, or the Devil according to Christian tradition
Sefer Yetsirah: the Hebrew Book of Creation
Sefiroth: the nine states of consciousness according to the Cabala
Shaman: a seer or mystic who enters the spirit word through a trance
Strwla: astrology
Swyno: to charm or enchant
Tabu: something forbidden or offensive to the gods
Talisman: model or carving used in ritual or carried for good luck
Totem: a sacred emblem or symbol, sometimes at the centre of a shrine
Voodoo: religious rituals invoking spirits through the use of magic
Wicca: the old religion involving witchcraft
Yr Hen Fachgen: The Old Boy (Devil)
Ysbryd drwg: evil spirit or devil
Yule: the old winter solstice festival, on 21 December
Zohar: The Book of Splendour (used by wizards)

Chapter Two --
Stories of the Pembrokeshire Wizards

From the foregoing it is apparent that there is a great "wizard tradition" in Pembrokeshire. Memories of most of the magicians or "knowing ones" have faded away, but some of them are remembered by name, and some of their stories are recounted below.

First there are a few stories of people with special powers who are immortalized in the ancient literature of Wales, including "The Mabinogion". In most of these stories the great heroes are tested through contact with wizards and their magic, and it is not always clear which of the characters in the tales actually have special powers. Most of the magic in these old tales is to do with enchantments, shape-changing and magic vessels or containers, and it is important to recognize that enchantment as it was understood in Celtic mythology did not include any concept of "the devil" or any concept of human beings making contact with a spirit world. These ideas came later, with the development of Christian theology. The inhabitants of Annwn were not spirits or ghosts but real people who simply lived in a world which was similar to our own in many respects but which was somewhat darker and more chaotic.

Ancient Enchantments

Pwyll and the Magic Bag

Pwyll the Prince of Dyfed was head over heels in love with Rhiannon, but having won her hand in marriage he lost it again before the wedding night. At the wedding feast he had probably had too much to drink, and when a young nobleman entered the hall and asked for a boon Pwyll replied without thinking "Whatever favour you ask of me, so long as it is in my power, you shall have it." Rhiannon was furious, for she recognized the young man as Gwawl, the one chosen by her father Hefeydd, against her will, to be her future husband. Sure enough, Gwawl asked for Rhiannon, and for the place of honour at the feast and marriage preparations. Pwyll knew that by his code of honour he was obliged to keep his promise and to give up his special place at Rhiannon's side.

However, Rhiannon was no ordinary princess, and she instantly devised a strategy to thwart the young man. When Pwyll replied that he would give all that was in his power to give, Gwawl was satisfied; but then Rhiannon told the young nobleman that the feast and the marriage preparations were hers to give, and that these things had already been given to Pwyll and his warriors and retainers from Dyfed. "But a year from tonight," she added, "a feast shall be prepared for you and your warriors in this court. Come then and you shall sleep with me." The young man was satisfied, and with an eager promise to return in a year's time he went on his way.

After this, the rest of the "wedding feast" was something of an anti-climax, with Pwyll depressed by his own stupidity and quite convinced that he would never marry Rhiannon. But the beautiful princess told him that all would be well; and before he left to return to Dyfed she gave him a small magic bag with detailed instructions as to what he should do in twelve months' time.

A year passed, and Pwyll and one hundred of his best warriors travelled on horseback under cover of darkness to the court of Rhiannon. When they arrived, the warriors dismounted and hid themselves in the orchard near the hall. From their hiding place they saw Gwawl and his retainers as they arrived. Then Rhiannon, as beautiful as ever, entered the hall in the company of her father. Later they heard the sounds of music and revelry as the marriage feast got under way.

Pwyll was hardly recognizable, with wild hair and beard and having dressed himself in the rough tattered clothes and rag boots of a vagabond. He waited until the feast was well advanced. Then, taking with him the little bag which Rhiannon had given him, he entered the hall and approached Gwawl and the princess at the head of the table. He saw that Rhiannon recognized him, but after the customary greetings he addressed the young nobleman. "God repay you for your greetings," he said. "I have a small request to make of you." Gwawl felt benevolent, and replied "I welcome your request, stranger. And if you ask me a reasonable boon, I will

Pwyll traps Gwawl in the magic bag -- one of many magical acts described in "The Mabinogion".

gladly give it to you." Then Pwyll held out the small bag and said "It is indeed a reasonable request, lord. I ask only that I may ward off hunger. The favour I ask is this small bag full of food." Gwawl replied at once, "That is a most modest request. You shall gladly have the food."

Then Gwawl instructed the attendants to bring meat, and bread, and fruit, and all manner of other foodstuffs, and to place them in the bag which Pwyll held open in front of him. But no matter how much food was placed inside it, it appeared no fuller than before. At last the servants wearied of the task, and Gwawl looked at the bag with amazement. "Friend," he asked, "will your bag never be full?" "Between me and God it will not," replied the whiskered and bedraggled Prince of Dyfed, "until a true nobleman who owns land and dominions shall arise and tread down the food in the bag with both feet, and shall say: Now the bag contains enough!"

At this Rhiannon intervened and said to Gwawl "Brave sir, rise up quickly, for you are such a man." Gwawl rose to the bait, jumped into the bag and began to tread down the food. But immediately the magic bag became larger. Pwyll pulled the top of the bag over Gwawl's head, tipped him over and fastened it with a knot. Then he pulled out a horn from his ragged tunic and blew a loud blast. At this signal, his warriors rushed into the hall and subdued the guests and retainers with ease, for they were in a mellow mood, having eaten and drunk far too much. Pwyll threw off his disguise, and he and his hundred warriors proceeded to play "badger in the bag." The bag, with poor Gwawl inside shrieking for mercy, was kicked and beaten with staves by every man in turn.

At last Hefeydd the Old, Rhiannon's father, intervened, for he was afraid that Gwawl would be killed. "It is not fitting for a nobleman to be slain inside a bag," he said. So Pwyll agreed to stop the game, and promised that he would abide by the decision of Rhiannon and her father concerning the battered young man. Gwawl was in no position to negotiate, and Rhiannon insisted that as a condition of his release he should give up his claim on her and should leave the hall with his chieftains and warriors, never to return. Further, she insisted that he should never lay claim or seek vengeance for what had happened to him. He also had to promise that he would pay sureties as a sign of good intent. And at last, all having been agreed, Gwawl was released from the magic bag to an accompaniment of hoots of derision. "I am bruised and wounded and in need of a bath," he complained. "And with your permission I will go on my way."

Covered with indignity, Gwawl mounted his horse and set off for home with his retinue, leaving only a few of his chieftains to pay the sureties and make other arrangements. Soon they set off too, leaving Pwyll and his warriors in full control of the situation. As they had done a year before, they took their places in the hall. Pwyll shaved and cut his hair, and took his place beside his beloved Rhiannon. The minstrels took up their instruments and began to play, and the feasting and drinking recommenced. The evening was passed in singing and laughter.

Then, a year later than planned, Pwyll and Rhiannon went to their bedchamber as man and wife. And there they passed the night in pleasure and contentment.

The Magical Abduction of Pryderi

When a son was born at Narberth to Pwyll and Rhiannon there was great rejoicing throughout Dyfed. Six nursemaids were appointed to keep a constant watch on the baby. But one night they became drowsy, and while they slept the boy disappeared. Fearful that they would be punished for betraying their trust, they decided to place the blame on the gentle and beautiful Rhiannon. Accordingly they killed a puppy and smeared its blood all over the baby's nursery. Then they went to Rhiannon, held her down and smeared blood on her hands and face. They told Pwyll and the court that she had killed the child and had struggled violently when they tried to subdue her. Strangely, their story was believed by the wise men of Dyfed.

Pwyll would not believe that Rhiannon had killed the baby, and he would not have her put away. But he had to submit to the judgment of the wise men or druids. They decreed that she was guilty, and devised a penance for her. She had to remain in the palace of Narberth for seven years, beside the mounting-block near the main gate; and there she should relate her story to all who came by, and offer to carry every visitor on her back through the palace entrance.

While Rhiannon had been giving birth to her son in Narberth, strange and magical things had been happening in Gwent, far away in the eastern corner of Wales. The Lord of Gwent was Teyrnon, who owned the best mare in the world. Every May Eve the mare gave birth to a foal, which immediately vanished. But Teyrnon decided that there was some magic involved, and that he would fight it. On this particular May Eve he brought the mare to the palace and kept watch on it. The mare gave birth to a fine colt, but at once Teyrnon heard a great noise like a storm, with a choir of wailing voices into the bargain. Then the huge arm of a monster came through the window and seized the newborn colt. But Teyrnon was ready for it. Quick as a flash he seized his sword and cut off the arm at the elbow. There was a fearsome roar, and Teyrnon rushed outside to see if he could catch sight of the creature. But it was too dark to see anything. When he returned he was amazed to see an infant boy in swaddling clothes in the straw next to the frightened colt.

The Lord of Gwent and his wife, satisfied that the enchantment was finished, decided to rear the mysterious child as their own. They christened him Gwri Gwallt Euryn (gold haired boy). He thrived and grew into a fine four-year-old, and on his birthday they gave him the colt that had been born on the same night as himself. Then the foster-parents heard from a traveller the sad story of Rhiannon. Teyrnon looked hard at the boy, and remembering the face of Pwyll from the time they had spent together in days gone by, he realized that Gwri must be Pwyll's missing son. He discussed matters with his wife, and they decided to return the boy to his real parents so that Rhiannon's terrible ordeal could be brought to an end.

So they set off for Narberth, with little Gwri riding on his own horse. When they arrived Rhiannon greeted them, but they refused to hear her story or to be carried on her back. They went into the palace, where Pwyll had prepared a magnificent feast for them. Teyrnon took the boy by the hand and set him before Pwyll, and told the story of his discovery and his childhood in Gwent. All those present, including the wise men of Dyfed, agreed that the likeness between Pwyll and Gwri was so striking that they could only be father and son.

Then Rhiannon was declared free of any guilt. Her penance was lifted from her and she was immediately restored to her position of honour at the right hand of the Prince of Dyfed. The boy with the golden hair was given the name his mother had given him when he was born -- Pryderi, which means Anxiety. Teyrnon and his wife returned to their own country, refusing the gifts offered by Pwyll and accepting only his offer of support and faithful friendship. And so the family was reunited in love and harmony, and Pryderi grew up to be a great Lord of Dyfed after his father.

Merlin and the Big Stones

Merlin or Myrddin is probably the best-known magician in the British tradition, made famous because he figures very large in the legends of King Arthur and the Knights of the Round Table. He is believed by some to have lived around the Sixth Century; by others to be an amalgam of various wizards who lived around that time; and by others to be a sheer fabrication. Whatever the truth of the matter, he was mentioned in the writings of Nennius in the

Eighth Century and by Geoffrey of Monmouth in the Twelfth Century, and thereafter by every author who chose to develop the Arthurian saga. However, he was not mentioned in the books of "The Mabinogion". The legends about him are scattered all over Wales, but legend has it that he was born near Carmarthen (Caerfyrddin or Merlin's Fort) and always looked on the Towy Valley as his real home. But what of Merlin's Hill and Merlin's Bridge in Haverfordwest? Maybe there is some folk memory of him in Pembrokeshire too.

One strange story links Merlin with the mystery of Stonehenge. It is said that many centuries ago King Aurelius Ambrosius was involved in a protracted war with the Irish. He decided that he would like to transport a spectacular ring of standing stones (called "The Giant's Ring") from the slopes of Mount Killaraus (near Kildare?) to Salisbury Plain, where he wanted to set it up as a great monument. He and his brother Uther Pendragon, and his princes and armies, tried over and again to remove the stones, but they were harried by their enemies and the stones proved to be too heavy for them. At last he called in Merlin the Magician, who scolded him for using brawn instead of brains, and proceeded to utter a magic incantation. Immediately the stones were uprooted, and flew through the air to be magically implanted in the chalky soil of Stonehenge. It was then dedicated as a memorial to dead heroes. A great feast was held, lasting three days, and Merlin was of course the toast of the party.

Local Wizards

John Harries of Cwrt-y-Cadno

The most famous of all the West Wales magicians were Dr John Harries of Cwrt-y-Cadno in Carmarthenshire and his son Henry who also carried on this strange trade. Both father and son were trained doctors and brilliant surgeons. There are innumerable stories about the special powers of "Old Dr Harries", in particular, in lifting curses, foretelling the future, solving mysteries and finding lost animals. He was reputed to be in touch with the spirit world, where his contacts brought him into grave danger on many occasions. Astrology was a particular interest of his, and he advertised his services in the local press for the calculation of nativities, fortunes and misfortunes, journeys, marriages, friends and enemies, sickness and death "deduced from the influence of the sun and moon, with the planetary orbs, at the time of birth." He claimed to be able to unravel the mysteries of clients' lives without even meeting them.

He was a skilled psychiatrist and a pioneer in the use of hypnosis, which he used with great success in the treatment of depressed and nervous patients. He was also remarkably clever in the performance of autopsies, and one of his hobbies was researching into the phenomena of extra-sensory perception. He also had a charming way with those who failed to pay their bills for consultation. He would normally send an invoice with a little note added, which read "Sir -- unless the above amount is paid to me on or before the due date, *adverse means will be resorted to*, for the recovery. Your humble servant, John Harries." This was not actually a threat of a curse, but it was near enough, and no doubt it was very effective!

John Harries died in 1839. According to one of the legends about him, the funeral was a strange affair, for the wizard had not wished for a Christian burial. The coffin with the great man's corpse in it was carried from the church to the grave, but afterwards all four bearers claimed that with every step taken towards the open grave the coffin became lighter and lighter, and they were all quite convinced that it was empty when it was let down into the hallowed ground. As a consequence the locals decided that the dead doctor had been mysteriously carried away by the Devil, right under their noses. It is said that after the funeral his books on witchcraft had to be burned in order to free his house from evil spirits. It is also claimed that the route followed by the funeral procession on its way to the church yard is still cold and ghostly, even on the warmest of summer days......

There is a strange Pembrokeshire dimension to the story of the passing of the old doctor. Early in the month of May, 1839, a man living near Nevern saw a most unusual death-light or canwyll gorff as he walked home one evening. This one was glowing with a light green colour as distinct from the death-lights normally reported from the parish, which were light blue in colour. The man knew that this must be the death light of somebody special. Accordingly he kept his ears open for news of a death in the neighbourhood. But then he heard that on 11th

May "Old Dr Harries" of Cwrt-y-Cadno had died, and he knew why the death light had been something special.

There are scores of stories about John Harries, and just a few of them are recounted in the following paragraphs. They will serve to give some indication of the awe in which he was held by his neighbours and by the wider West Wales community.

Trouble with the Law

The case which brought Dr Harries his first recognition in the community involved a quite difficult confrontation with the law. Around the year 1800 a young woman of Llandeilo disappeared. She was engaged to be married, and her sweetheart and family searched high and low for her without success. Many of the neighbours also helped, and requests for information were sent out over a wide area. No evidence of her whereabouts could be found. At last her parents went to see Dr Harries at Cwrt-y-Cadno. At that time he did not have any great reputation, but he had helped some people with their problems, and the poor demented parents had to try every possible avenue that might lead them to a solution of their terrible mystery.

On hearing the details, Dr Harries consulted his magic books and then informed them as follows. The poor girl, he said, was dead. She had been murdered by her sweetheart, and was buried in the mid-day shade of a certain tree. He did not know the name of the place, but he could describe it exactly. The tree stood alone near a brook, and in the hollow of the tree there was a bee's nest.

The poor parents were naturally horrified to hear this news, but when Dr Harries had consoled them as best he could, they returned home and instituted a further search. Neighbours scoured the countryside around Llandeilo until they found the spot described by the magician, and there, in the mid-day shadow of the tree described by the wizard, they found a shallow grave containing the body of the murdered girl. The murderer had fled, but he was eventually found and arrested. He confessed to the crime, and was in due course executed.

When the court case was complete, the legal authorities took it into their heads to charge Dr Harries with being an accomplice to the crime, for they could not conceive of any way in which he could have known the girl's burial place other then through direct involvement. Local people were outraged, for they were perfectly prepared to believe that the doctor was a "knowing one". But in the face of much local hostility the magistrates, Mr Lloyd of Glansevin and Mr Glyn of Glanbran, persisted. They summoned the doctor to the magistrates court in Llandovery, where he was duly charged. But there was not a scrap of evidence against him. When the proceedings dragged on, Dr Harries at last started to get angry with the stupid questions which the magistrates were asking. He said "Your Honours, I fear that we are getting nowhere in this matter. If you wish me to demonstrate my powers for you, I suggest we do the following. If you will both tell me the date and the hour on which you were born, I will tell you immediately the date and the hour upon which you will die."

At this, the magistrates both came out in a cold sweat. They suddenly decided that the matter had gone far enough, and dismissed the case. Dr Harries returned to Cwrt-y-Cadno a local hero, with his reputation well and truly made.

The Case of the Missing Cows

One story of wizardry which was very well known in Pembrokeshire tells of a farmer from the Pendine area who lost three cows. Having searched in vain for them, he went at last to see Dr John Harries at Cwrt-y-Cadno. The great consuriwr or magician listened intently to his story, but then said that he could not solve the problem immediately. He would need a little time, he said, to consult his magic books and his contacts in the spirit world. He suggested that the farmer should find lodgings in the neighbourhood for the night, and then come back next morning. This the farmer agreed to do.

Having taken his leave of the great man, the farmer was wondering where he might find some accommodation. But then, in crossing the yard outside Dr Harries' house, he noticed a barn nearby which looked as if it might provide him with a nice dry bed for the night. He looked inside, and found that it was half full of sweet dry hay. So he settled down quietly in the hay and eventually went to sleep.

About one o'clock in the morning the farmer was awakened by the footsteps of Dr Harries coming into the barn. He carried a lantern in his hand, which he put down on the floor in the middle of a clearing in the hay. The farmer hardly dared to breathe, and snuggled down deeply into the hay for fear of being discovered. But then, as he watched, Dr Harries drew a circle around himself in the dust of the barn floor, opened a big magic book, and made an incantation which had the effect of summoning seven spirits. They came one by one, in the shapes of assorted animals and humans and strange demons; and as each one appeared he asked "Where are the farmer's missing cows?" Some of the spirits appeared quite stupid, and the doctor became irritated with them when they gave no help at all. One of the spirits, when asked the question, replied "A pig in the hay". This made the farmer greatly alarmed, since he was convinced that Dr Harries would take the hint and discover him in his hiding-place. But he did not, and the tense moment passed.

At last the seventh spirit, on being pressed by the doctor, shouted out "The farmer's cows will be on Carmarthen Bridge at twelve of the clock tomorrow." Satisfied at last, the doctor smiled and dismissed all the spirits. Then he stepped outside the circle, picked up his lantern, and went off to bed.

The spirits came one by one, in the shapes of assorted wild animals and ferocious humans.

The farmer was so excited that he could not sleep. He now knew the answer to his problem, and thought that he might as well save on the magician's fee; so as soon as he saw the first light of dawn driving the darkness from the eastern sky he crept out and hurried back to Carmarthen. It was a long walk, but he got there just before noon. As predicted, his three cows were crossing the bridge, driven by a stranger who was intent upon selling them at Carmarthen market. He challenged the man, who ran off. Delighted, he turned the cows round and started to drive them homewards.

However, he had progressed no more than half a mile when all three cows collapsed at the side of the road, more dead than alive. The farmer, whose conscience had been troubling him about evading the magician's fee, became convinced that the cows were bewitched. So he had to leave the animals where they were and make the long trek all the way back to Cwrt-y-Cadno. The doctor was waiting for him. "Serve thee right," he said, wagging his finger. "I have bewitched thy cattle as a punishment for running away without paying me for my information from the spirit world. Now, if you pay me, all will be well with thy three cows." The farmer had no option but to pay the fee, and on returning to the cows he found them on their feet, happily eating buttercups at the side of the road.

Joseph Harries of Werndew

The best-known soothsayer or *dyn hysbys* in Pembrokeshire in the early years of the nineteenth century was Dr Joseph Harries of Werndew, near Dinas. He was sometimes confused in folk memory with Abe Biddle who lived near Haverfordwest and with John Harries of Cwrt-y-cadno. He was well known for his remarkable powers and for his ability as a healer. He could foretell the future, but he also had a mastery of the occult.

Although he was best known in the Fishguard area his fame spread all over Pembrokeshire and even further afield. Some people believed that he was in league with the devil, but there are no tales of him doing evil and indeed he seems to have had a substantial reputation for righting wrongs and assisting in the recovery of lost animals from local farms.

Werndew still exists, and the house is still inhabited. It is located about one kilometre east of Dinas Cross, and is reached via a track and public right of way on the south side of the A487 trunk road.

The Case of the Stolen Painting

Stolen property seems to have been a particular specialty as far as Dr Harries was concerned. One day a wealthy woman came up the track to Werndew in her carriage and reported to the wizard that a very valuable painting which had hung in her house had disappeared. There were no signs of a burglar entering the house, and no damage had been done. On hearing the story from his client, Joseph at once suspected an "inside job." So he got out his magic mirror, and said to the lady "Now let's see together what we can do!"

The two of them sat in the living room and watched the mirror. After a time, an image appeared in the mirror and the lady exclaimed that she recognized a very good friend of the family. She could hardly believe that such a person could have been guilty of the theft, but she confirmed to Joseph that the family was in financial difficulties and that her friend might have been driven by desperation to the theft of the painting. No doubt she hoped to travel to London with it and to sell it there.

Having asked his client for the name of the culprit, Joseph wrote it onto a piece of paper, and pierced it with a needle. He then turned to the lady and said "Your friend will now start to feel ill, and she will know that if she does not return the painting immediately she will be eaten up with a strange disease. I suggest, Madam, that you now go home and await developments." The lady was somewhat taken aback by this turn of events, but she agreed to do as Dr Harries suggested. She took her leave of the good doctor, returned to her coach and clattered off down the track towards Dinas. She lived a fair distance away, and by the time she arrived home half an hour had passed. As she alighted from her coach she was met by one of her servants, who handed to her a large flat parcel wrapped up in brown paper. He said that a strange horseman with a great scarf over his face had ridden up to the house at high speed just a few minutes before, and had left the parcel without saying a word before galloping off again. Naturally enough, when the lady opened the parcel, she found her precious painting inside.

A week later the lady and her guilty friend met socially, and the lady asked after her health. "Oh, I feel much better, thank you," replied the friend, with a flush upon her cheek. "I had been planning a trip to London, but a week ago I suddenly came over feeling very ill, and had to cancel my plans. But I have been getting better gradually, and now I feel quite well again."

William John's Aerial Journey

William John lived at Trewern, about a mile from Pontfaen. His wife fell seriously ill with inflammation of the lungs, and it transpired that the local doctor could do little to help. William became desperately worried as her health deteriorated, and at last it was suggested by neighbours that he should go to see the famous magician Dr Joseph Harries of Werndew. It was too dark to take his horse, so William had to walk all the way, down into the Gwaun Valley, up the other side and over the wild moor of Mynydd Melyn.

At last he arrived, very late at night. He hammered on the door of the doctor's cottage, and the famous man let him in. He listened intently to William's account of his wife's symptoms, and immediately poured some special potion into a small bottle. He gave it to William. "Now," he said. "Get back to your wife as fast as you possibly can, for she is close to death even as I speak." William's heart sank. "I will, sir," he replied, "But the road is in a bad state, and the old footpath over Mynydd Melyn is even worse. There is no moon, and I can hardly see where I am going." The doctor nodded. "All right," he said. "Make your way as best you can to the top of the lane past Bryn, and then you will have a lift."

William John puffed and panted up the muddy lane, and when he reached the top he was utterly surprised and bewildered to be lifted upward and carried along through the air by some mysterious force. When he reached Trewern he looked at his pocket watch and discovered that his aerial journey in the pitch darkness over a distance of 5 miles had taken only a few minutes. He was just in time to give the medicine to his wife, who had only a spark of life left in her. The medicine worked like magic, and very soon she was restored to full health.

Joseph and the Hornets

During the winter of 1803 there was an evening party for gentlemen in a north Pembrokeshire vicarage. Joseph Harries was among the guests. There were many clergymen present, and a good time was had by all, with fine food, singing, telling of tales and much laughter. At last, in the early hours, the conversation drifted round to the occult. Joseph said nothing, for his strange powers were well known, but one elderly cleric denounced all sorcery and witchcraft (rheibio) as evil trickery, and of course it was incumbent upon all the other clerics present to nod gravely in agreement.

At last Joseph got up, disappeared through the French doors onto the lawn, and returned holding three small rings. He held them up, saying quietly to the assembled company "Now, gentlemen, we'll see what is possible." He placed the three rings on the floor, left the room and locked the door on the outside, leaving the trapped clerics and their guests to stare intently at the rings. Suddenly, in one of the rings, a small buzzing insect appeared. It looked like a fly, but as the men watched it grew and grew into a large angry hornet. It flew into another ring and was replaced by a second fly in the first ring. This also turned into a huge hornet. As they watched with mounting alarm the process speeded up until the room was filled with droning hornets. Eventually the ceiling was darkened with the creatures and panic set in as they flew into men's hair and clothes, into the curtains and furniture. As the men shouted and fought to escape from the room the wizard suddenly opened the door. In an instant the hornets swarmed out towards the darkness and droned away into the distance. Joseph said nothing, but picked the rings up off the floor. He knew that he had spoiled the party, but thereafter all the clerics present became somewhat more cautious in their pronouncements concerning matters beyond their understanding.

Joseph and the Missing Jewels

One day Dr Harries was called in by a countess who was staying at the mansion of a wealthy Pembrokeshire family. The doctor duly arrived, and impressed the lady with his appearance. He was a tall, slender man with long shaggy hair and large, deep-set eyes, and a somewhat dreamy expression on his face. But his voice was well modulated and his manner courteous, and this gave the lady some confidence that he might be able to help her with a matter that required the utmost discretion.

The countess described to the wizard how she had lost some of her jewels, and she declared that they had been safely in her travelling bag when she had left another Pembrokeshire mansion at dawn the previous day. On hearing the story Joseph opened his battered old bag and took out a mirror, which he placed on the table in front of the countess. Then he asked her to look into it and to tell him what she saw. She sat down and looked into the mirror while Joseph asked her to "compose herself". At last she said that she could see nothing but a mist, which she described as like the steam from a boiler. "Good, good. Now look again", said the doctor. And as she looked quietly into the mirror the mist rolled away and she saw a woman in a dress of white brocade, with her back turned towards her. "Do you know her?" asked Joseph. "I don't think so," replied the countess, "but I cannot see her face, for her back is turned." The doctor then told her to pause for a while, and to close her eyes. This she did. After a few minutes of silence she was asked to open her eyes again and to look once more into the mirror.

And now, as the countess looked, the woman in the mirror turned to face her, and she was amazed to see some of her jewels in her hands, and others upon her neck and in her hair. Again the doctor asked "Do you know her?" And the countess instantly recognized her as a personal friend of her hostess, from whom she had recently taken her leave.

Joseph was then asked to undertake discreet investigations, which he did with considerable tact. The result was the restoration of the jewels to their rightful owner. The thief was never prosecuted, but the solving of the mystery made a profound impression upon a small circle of the Pembrokeshire gentry.

Abe Biddle of Millin Dingle

Abe (or Aby) Biddle lived in the early part of the Nineteenth Century in Millin Dingle, not far from Picton Castle and the Rhos. Today there is not much left of the small community which once clustered around the head of the tidal creek of the Millin Brook - - a bridge, an ancient crossroads, a small chapel, a quarry and a farm. But there must have been a mill and an inn here at one time, and old maps show that there were some cottages in the woods. Abe must have lived in one of these cottages, now reduced to rubble. We have only one description of what he looked like. Apparently he was a big man with long hair, and when he moved about he used a stout walking stick. But he was tidily dressed, and he had an efficient and courteous manner. Visitors to his cottage were interested to see that he lived in "a sort of cosy simplicity."

Abe Biddle and the Cartlett Mill Mystery

Once upon a time the manager of the Cartlett corn mill (in Haverfordwest) became convinced that one of his staff was systematically stealing quantities of flour. He could not be sure, and so one day he laid a trap by making a careful note of the number of sacks stored at the end of the day's work. Sure enough, next morning one of the sacks was missing. He had his suspicions as to who was responsible, but none of the staff would say anything and he had no evidence to go on. There was nothing for it but to consult Abe Biddle, the Wise Man of Millin Dingle, who lived not far outside the town. On hearing the story, the wizard said that he already knew the culprit. "Leave it to me," he said. "Go back to the mill, and next time a sack is stolen the person responsible will be marked for all to see."

Sure enough, some days later the manager discovered that another sack of flour had disappeared. Immediately he summoned all his workers to line up against a wall, and noticed that one of the women had part of her face covered with a thick head-scarf. He challenged her to remove it, and she reluctantly obeyed, to reveal a strange "excrescence" of skin on her cheek. The miserable woman said that it had suddenly appeared, and some of her fellow workers remarked that it had the shape of a sack of flour. On being pressed by the manager, she confessed to the thefts from the mill. She was immediately dismissed, and the strange mark on her face did not disappear till she had paid for all of the flour which she had stolen.

Abe and the Church Window

Saturday night was a time of heavy drinking in the village of Hubberston. One Sunday morning the congregation of Hubberston Church turned up for Matins to discover that the beautiful east window of the church had been smashed in. The parishioners were distraught, and although suspicion fell on several local persons who were renowned for their love of the bottle, no evidence was to be found as to the guilty party. The church wardens met together to discuss the matter, and someone suggested that a deputation should be sent to Abe Biddle at Millin Dingle. The vicar agreed, and so off they went to see him.

Abe welcomed the men into his little cottage, He invited them to sit down and asked them to tell their story. He listened intently, and then he went to the corner of the room and fetched his magic mirror. He placed it before them, and as they watched in silence a face appeared in the glass, first very faintly and then with some clarity. Immediately the men recognized the face as that of a local man who had long held a grudge against the vicar. "Maybe we cannot get recompense for the broken window," they said. "But can you help in bringing the wickedness of this deed home to the villain and in ensuring that he feels some remorse?"

"Just leave the matter in my hands," said Abe. "I'll both bring the deed home to his heart, and also mete out to him a proper punishment." And so the men from Hubberston took their leave and went on their way.

On the following Sunday morning, as the good people of the village were present at Matins, the service was interrupted by a great commotion outside. Through the windows the parishioners could see a man rushing aimlessly and wildly back and forth on the bank close to the church. The bank was covered in thick gorse bushes, but the man rushed back and forth through the bushes, apparently unable to stop himself. Every now and then he squealed like a stuck pig or shrieked like a demon as he tripped and fell headlong into one or other of the gorse bushes. The astonishment of the congregation at last turned to consternation, as the good people feared that the man would seriously hurt himself. But at last he ran madly into the church. He rushed up the aisle, and then fell onto his knees in front of the altar, gasping for breath and covered with cuts and scratches. There, in a loud voice, he confessed that it was he who had smashed the church window while in a drunken stupor, and he begged the vicar and the congregation for pardon.

Needless to say, the priest and congregation showed their Christian charity and forgave the poor man, who had clearly suffered enough for his crime. Thenceforth he became a regular church member and a good Christian gentleman.

John Adolph's Mercy Mission

John Adolph lived at Garron Pill, one of the creeks on the eastern shore of the Daugleddau River. His little daughter was seriously ill, and John feared for her life. He became quite convinced that she had been bewitched by the famous black witches who lived at Garron. No-one could help her, and at last John was advised by a friend to go and see Abe Biddle in his cottage at Millin Dingle.

On his way to see the wise man, John hurt his foot, and he was limping quite badly by the time he reached Abe's cottage. He knocked on the door and was invited inside, and the great man listened in silence to the story of the little girl's illness. Then Abe mixed up a bottle of medicine for the child, and gave it to the worried father. He then urged John to hurry home as fast as he could go, for he said that the girl was very close to death. At this, John became desperately concerned. "To hurry, Sir, is my reasonable duty," he said. "But to reach home soon is quite out of the question, the road being so rough and my foot being injured." "I suppose you are right," said Abe. "But don't you worry, for I'll give you a lift. Good night!" And with that he disappeared back into the cottage and closed the door.

John Adolph set off on his way, hurrying up the hill above the dingle and limping badly. In a cold sweat and fearing for the life of his daughter he looked at his watch and saw that it was a quarter to ten. After a couple of minutes he reached the top of the hill and came to a crossroads. As he approached he saw a magnificent white horse, saddled and bridled, trotting towards him. Remembering Abe's parting words and believing that he was meant to use the horse, John pulled himself into the saddle and grasped the reins. Then the creature arched its neck and with a shrill neigh it was away. John had never ridden such a majestic beast. He felt that he was flying, and he had no sensation of the horse touching the ground. It galloped so swiftly that John could hardly breathe. Below him he saw the muddy estuary of the Eastern Cleddau at Landshipping. At last, after only a few minutes John saw his house below him, and the horse descended at Garron Gate, only about one hundred yards from the Pill. John dismounted, and he watched as the horse cantered off up the road, to disappear in a sheet of flame.

Then the creature arched its neck, and with a shrill neigh it was away.

John rushed into the house and quickly gave the medicine to his little daughter who was now hardly breathing and was obviously close to death. Immediately the little girl began to breathe more easily, and John was able to relax. Then he looked at his watch, and he discovered that it was eight minutes to ten. Only seven minutes had passed since he had last looked at his watch, and he had travelled a distance of six miles over land and water on the back of the white horse. The journey itself could not have lasted for more than four minutes.

After this the little girl quickly recovered, and John remained grateful to Abe Biddle for the rest of his life. He never forgot the white horse, but he never saw it again.

Wil Tiriet of Caerfarchell

Around 1830-1850 a tailor called William Howells lived in the hamlet of Caerfarchell, near Middle Mill,. He was widely known as Wil Tiriet or Wiliet, and he had special powers. In Welsh he was known as a *dyn hysbys* or soothsayer, and two stories survive which reveal how he could look into the future.

The Death of Young William Jones
The old Baptist chapel at Middle Mill had a substantial congregation in the middle of the Nineteenth Century – large enough to demand the pastoral care of two ministers. The older of the two, John Reynolds, was well known in Baptist circles throughout West Wales; his young assistant was called William Jones. One day Wil Tiriet prophesied that the younger man would soon die. The whole community was thrown into confusion by this prediction – some people were outraged, some were terrified, some were angry, and others were sceptical. As if in answer to those who professed not to believe him, Wil Tiriet further prophesied that at the funeral of William Jones there would be a minister with a very long white beard. Since nobody knew of a white-bearded minister in the district everybody assumed that Wil's eerie predictions could not possibly come true.

In a few weeks William Jones was dead. On the day of the funeral the cortege started from the young minister's house and made its slow way to the chapel. They arrived and entered, and there, sitting in the big pew, was a reverend gentleman with a long white beard. He was Dr Thomas Davies, the principal of the Haverfordwest Baptist College, who had rushed on horseback to the funeral. He had lost much time because his horse had cast a shoe; and so, being too late to attend the gathering at the house of the deceased, he had gone straight to the chapel ahead of the rest of the mourners.

Wil Tiriet and the Nolton Coffin

Once upon a time, about 1830, Wil Tiriet of Caerfarchell was chatting to one of his neighbours, a carpenter named Francis John. He told him that there would soon be a funeral of a young man at Fachelich, a hamlet about two miles away. The carpenter laughed at him, for none of the young men of Fachelich was known to be ill, but the soothsayer insisted "Thou'llt believe it when thy brother and thou carry his coffin past the doctor's house on the road to Fachelich." The matter was quickly forgotten.

Then there came a report of a sailor being drowned near Nolton Haven, whose body had been washed ashore. The dead man proved to be from Fachelich, and Francis John and his brother Bill were asked to make the coffin. They had to carry it all the way to Nolton. It was a long walk, and the coffin was heavy, and having remembered Wil Tiriet's prophecy Francis determined to prove him wrong by getting two other neighbours to give a hand. The men were to take it turn and turn about, but there was some confusion and in the argument about whose turn was next Wil's prophecy was forgotten about. Sure enough, when the coffin was carried past the doctor's door it was carried by Francis and Bill, with the other two men walking behind.

John Jenkin of Nevern

There are a number of strange stories connected with Nevern, some of them relating to magic and the occult. For example, it is believed that John Jenkin (Ioan Siengcyn), who was the schoolmaster in Nevern around 1780, was not only a poet but also a conjuror or *consuriwr* who could summon up evil spirits.

Inside the Magic Circle

One day a pupil of Nevern School asked Mr Jenkin whether it would be possible for him to see the Devil. "You may see him", said the master, "if you have the courage for it. But I do not choose to call him until I have work for him to do." So the boy waited. Not long afterwards, a man came to the master; he reported the theft of some money, and asked if he could help him to identify the culprit. "Now," said the master to the pupil, "I have some work for the Devil."

Next night, John Jenkin led the boy out into the wood and drew a circle on the ground, so that they both stood inside the circle. Then the master called an evil spirit by its name. A light appeared in the sky, and it shot like a bolt of lightning down to the circle. Then, as it moved around the outside of the circle, the conjuror asked it who had stolen the man's money; the evil spirit replied that it did not know, and disappeared. Then the schoolmaster called another evil spirit by name; and presently they saw the resemblance of a bull flying through the air, as fierce and ferocious as could be imagined, and it too landed outside the circle. The bull was asked who had stolen the money, but it did not know; and so it too disappeared.

By now the boy was almost fainting with fright, and the schoolmaster waited considerately for a while for him to recover his wits. Then he called for a third spirit. This time a spirit dressed in white came out of the shadows of the wood, and moved quietly around the circle. "Ah," said the conjuror, "this is better! Now we shall get to the bottom of this." And sure enough, the spirit spoke to the master in a language the boy did not understand. Then it disappeared in a ball of red fire.

After this, John Jenkin correctly told the man who had stolen his money, and it was recovered. But the boy was so frightened by the episode that he was in poor health for many years afterwards.

Some other Wizards

The Cunning Man of Pentregethin

Once upon a time there was a strange old man who lived in a house called Pentregethin or Pentregethen. He was believed to be a wizard, and nowadays he would perhaps be known as a diviner, spiritualist or seer. His reputation locally was much greater than that of parsons or conventional doctors, and there are still vague memories of his "wonderful actions" in ascertaining the state of health of absent friends and performing inexplicable deeds.

The Cunning Man was most famous for his ability to control the weather, and he was able to sell either fair winds or foul winds to his clients. Sailors often came to him before embarking on a voyage in order to buy favourable winds, but unfortunately he seemed to prefer to sell foul winds to those who wished harm to come upon either sailors or local sailing vessels. For this reason he was assumed to be more closely in touch with evil spirits than with those who provided protection.

It may be assumed that The Cunning Man practiced his strange and deadly craft in the latter part of the Eighteenth Century. Maybe he had something to do with the terrible wreck of the *Phoebe and Peggy* in 1773, or the disaster linked with the plunder at Druidston of the wreck of the *Increase* in 1791? Other vessels sunk in St Bride's Bay in the same period were the *John and Michael* (1794) and the *Rose* (1795). We know of the wreck of the *Morva* in 1793 off St David's Head, and the full-rigged ship *Providence* near the North Bishop Rock in 1797. But most of these vessels were sailing neither to nor from Pembrokeshire ports. We may suppose that The Cunning Man worked mostly on the fate of local small trading ships or fishing boats sailing out of Porth Clais, Solva, Fishguard or Abercastle. Many of these were lost with all hands and without trace, victims of the cruel stormy seas around the Pembrokeshire coast. And many of these losses were never even recorded in the port books of the day, giving rise to strange and dark tales of intervention by the man who lived at Pentregethin.

Old Levi Salmon of Cilgwyn

Around 1880 an old man called Levi Salmon was well known in the Newport (Pembs) area as a *dyn hysbys* or magician. He was also referred to as "Dr Cwac". He lived in the house called Plas y Ffynnon, not far from Temple Bar. One day a neighbour from Cilgwyn, who happened to have some fine plum trees in his garden, called in a state of some agitation to see Old Levi. It was a fine warm September, and there was a heavy crop of plums on the trees, but the neighbour complained that somebody was getting into the garden and stealing the plums whenever he was out in the fields. He had a pretty good idea who the culprit was – a young man called Tom who lived nearby and who had a reputation for thieving. But he had no proof, and now he called on Levi to give him some help. "Just leave it to me," said the old man mysteriously. "You won't be troubled any more."

Next day Levi's neighbour was out in the field working on the corn harvest when he heard a terrible commotion coming from the direction of his garden. Somebody was shouting and screaming as if in mortal danger, and the neighbour immediately ran back to see what was going on. As he arrived home, he caught a glimpse of young Tom rushing off down the lane, screaming that he was being attacked by adders. When he got home he was in a state of shock, and admitted to his parents that he had gone into the garden to pinch a few plums, only to find when he got there that he was surrounded by a writhing mass of adders. He had not been bitten, but the shock was enough to put the lad off stealing for the rest of his life.

After this, there were no more thefts of plump plums from the neighbour's garden, and he could not help reflecting on the fact that he never saw an adder in his garden before, or after, that fine day in September.

William Gwyn and his Magic Book

We know remarkably little about William Gwyn apart from the fact that as a young man he was not too skilled in his craft. He lived at a place called Olmws or Holmus near Little Newcastle. Not far away was the River Afon Anghof, which ran down from Mynydd Preseli. One fine day he was sitting on the bank of the river consulting his magic book, and he decided that he would try to summon up a familiar spirit. He followed the instructions carefully, and suddenly a terrible demon appeared out of thin air. In a thunderous voice it demanded to know what task it should undertake. William was at first greatly taken aback, but he knew that evil spirits had to be set to work as soon as they appeared; and he also knew that they would always obey instructions. He was quick-witted enough to say to the demon "Go back to my house and fetch the riddle from my coal-shed! And then come back here and empty the river with it!" So the demon rushed off and returned with the riddle, and set to work with ferocious energy in trying to empty the river. Water flew in all directions, and the demon managed only to deepen one pool in the river.

William had not read so far in his book that he knew how to get rid of demons, but while the demon continued with its futile task he was able to find the correct instructions. These he gave to the demon in a loud voice, and it promptly disappeared. William was greatly relieved, and after that he was very cautious in the matter of summoning up spirits. Later on, one of the village boys pointed out to William how much deeper the trout pool had become, but William simply smiled a mysterious smile.

Chapter Three
Tales of the Pembrokeshire Witches

Moll of Redberth

Moll of Redberth was a famous witch who lived in the early Nineteenth Century in a little cottage on the road from Carew to Begelly. Many stories were in circulation in the Carew area about her evil powers, and there is no doubt that most of the local people were frightened of her. After she died it was said that she had confessed on her deathbed to the parish priest that she had been a witch for 37 years. She confessed to having harmed scores of people with her spells, and told the priest how she had acquired her occult powers. Apparently, as a young woman attending her first communion service in Carew Cheriton church, she had not eaten the bread but had kept it in her hand. Then, on the way home from church, she had fed the sacred bread to a dog on the road. "I thus gave unto Satan the body of my Lord," she said. "And in return he gave to me the power to bewitch." There are many other stories in the literature of women who "sold their souls" in a similar way, and there is no doubt that the use of a tabu object (such as a piece of consecrated bread) for a profane or humdrum purpose was assumed to lead the perpetrator straight to Hell!

Moll uses the Evil Eye

In the shearing season of 1841 Moll went to a farmer near Carew to ask if she could have a little fleece with which to spin some woollen yarn. The farmer refused, since Moll was always begging for things, and the old woman went on her way muttering threats. "Just you wait," she said. "You will soon wish you had been more civil with me, for something terrible is about to happen." The farmer watched her as she went up the farm lane. He saw that she stopped at a field gate, opened it and went into the field.

Then she counted carefully the sheep that were in the field. There were 31 fine ewes, all newly shorn. She looked at them carefully, then left the field, closed the gate and went on her way.

By the evening all 31 sheep were dead. The farmer was distraught, since they were extremely valuable animals, but there was nothing he could do. How could he prove to anybody that Moll was responsible? But to his dying day he claimed that Old Moll had cast "the evil eye" onto his sheep, and that the blame lay entirely at her door.

An old woodcut showing a house occupied by a witches' coven. A man peeping through a hole in the door sees the witches leaving via the chimney prior to flying off on their broomsticks.

Moll and the Bucket of Culm

It was a dark and drizzly day in November 1842, with a cold wind blowing in from the west. Billy Morris of Dairy Hays, on the edge of the hamlet of Carew Cheriton, was not looking forward to a long journey which he knew would leave him wet and miserable, but his culm supply was almost finished, and he had to go to Bonville's Court Colliery for another cart-load if he was to keep the home fire burning. So he prepared his heavy cart, harnessed his two best cart-horses, put on his waterproofs and set off for Saundersfoot.

Billy bought his culm from the pit-head at a reasonable price and set off for home with the drizzle still swirling about him. The load was heavy and the five-mile journey slow. At last he reached Redberth, and with less than two miles to go he allowed himself the luxury of thinking about his warm fireside. As he passed through the village he saw Old Moll standing at the door of her clom cottage. She begged him to give her a bucketful of culm for her fire; but he was in a hurry to get home and he ignored her as he drove past. He knew that Old Moll was a witch, but he was in no mood to mollify her since she was always asking for things and never gave anything in return.

He had not gone fifty yards up the road when the cart tipped over backwards, flinging him off his driving seat and depositing the whole load of culm in the middle of the road. At the same time the cart-horse harnesses came loose, freeing the two horses, upon which they galloped off into the distance. Billy was furious, and chased off after them, shaking his fist in the air and shouting at the top of his voice. At this Moll quietly came out of her cottage with a bucket and a little shovel. She filled the bucket with culm and went back inside.

When Billy at last returned, having collected his two cart-horses, he discovered that the back end of the cart was broken. Feeling fed up to the back teeth, he harnessed up the horses again and started to load the culm back onto the damaged cart with his big shovel. While he was in the middle of his heavy labour Old Moll came out of her cottage again and looked on with a grin on her face. "I suppose ye don't mind that I helped meself to a bucket of culm just now, Billy," she said. "I sees that thy cart is summat smaller than t'was, an' won't hold so much culm, so I thought I'd save yer from havin' two journeys to fetch it home."

Moll and the Bewitched Cream

Sarah Cole lived at a cottage called The Bog, not far from Upper Nash. She kept three cows and churned her milk every week, taking 6 lbs of butter quite regularly to Pembroke Market, where she exchanged it for groceries. One fine morning, as she was putting some fresh cream into the churn, Old Moll called at the door, begging. Sarah had no time for the old woman, for she had work to do, and she turned her away. Moll said not a word, but she was mortally offended, and immediately "cast the evil eye" on the cream. When she had gone Sarah started the churning, but on this occasion the tedious work went on and on all day without the cream even beginning to separate. At dusk Sarah was feeling exhausted and had to give up the task, having made no progress at all in setting the butter. She became quite convinced that Old Moll had cast a spell on her cream.

Sarah went outside into the back-yard in order to get some fresh air, and there, in the fading daylight, she was surprised to see on her gatepost a black glutinous mass which was known to country people as "witches' butter". (Nowadays we know it to be a fungus, with the Latin name *Exida tremella*.) On seeing this Sarah knew what to do, for she had heard about witches' butter from her parents. She knew that the strange black substance was a part of the spell that Old Moll had cast on her cream. She went back into the house, heated up her poker in the fire until it was white hot, and then she attacked the enemy. As she thrust the poker into the witches' butter it spat and hissed and then dissolved into a cloud of foul-smelling steam. This broke the spell. Sarah heard a strange groaning noise as the evil power was broken; and then she heard a loud commotion like the flapping wings of a large bird.

Confident that the evil power had now departed, Sarah returned to her churning, and in no time at all she had a quantity of excellent butter to take to Pembroke Market next day.

Dolly, Nansi and the Others

The Queen of the Pembrokeshire Witches

Dolly Llewellin was known as the Queen of the Pembrokeshire witches, and she was widely feared in the area around Carew Newton. She lived in a cottage on Rosemary Lane. One Saturday evening she was coming home from Pembroke market with a heavy basket full of provisions. Mr and Mrs Lloyd of Carew Newton were driving home along the same road in their heavily-laden trap, and they passed Dolly at Penny Bridge near Holyland. William Evans the blacksmith overheard the following conversation.

"Come now," said Dolly to Mr Lloyd, "take me up, for I have a heavy basket." Mr Lloyd replied "I cannot, for I have a heavily laden trap as it is." "Ha!" she exclaimed in disgust, and asked him a second time. The reply was the same, as it was after a third request. At last she turned away and said "So be it then. The devil take you!"

Mr and Mrs Lloyd continued up the hill towards Holyland House, but near the entrance gate of the mansion the linch pin fell out and the wheel dropped off the trap. The farmer and his wife were flung onto the road, and flour and groceries were scattered about over a wide area. William Evans helped them to clear up the mess and to get things back into the trap, and the wheel was secured in position. Mr Lloyd was furious. "You damned thundering old witch!" he shouted, taking up his horse whip. "If you don't take the curse off me this minute I'll murder you!" Dolly didn't look in the least abashed, and there followed a period of negotiation. At last he agreed to give her a lift if she said "God bless you!". This she did, somewhat reluctantly, and the curse having been lifted in this way the trap and its three occupants made the rest of the journey back to Carew Newton quite uneventfully.

Tom Eynon the Witch

Tom Eynon was feared by almost everybody. He lived at The Rock, near Lamphey, and it was well known that if you happened to get on the wrong side of him he was quite likely to "cast the evil eye" on you, leading to endless trouble. There were various tales in circulation around 1840, one of which involved a bewitching of a butter churn. But then things rebounded on Tom, much to the delight of the locals.

Tom was married twice. He treated his first wife very harshly, and never gave her sufficient money to pay for food and other household needs. The poor woman led a miserable existence, and matters were not helped by the way in which most of the locals kept well clear of her husband. When she died, Tom waited for a respectable period of time and then he married again. The locals felt sorry for the new wife, assuming that the poor woman would have just as miserable a time as her predecessor.

Right in the middle of the wedding night, at a very embarrassing moment, who should appear next to the bed but the very angry ghost of Tom's first wife. "Tom! Tom!" she cried. "Give me some money, give me some money!" Tom's new wife was terrified by the apparition and fled downstairs. Tom was very angry but perhaps not very surprised, since he had frequent encounters with the spirit world. He knew how to get rid of ghosts, and drove the phantom away. However, nothing would induce his new wife to return to bed that night, and indeed she was so frightened by the experience that it took many weeks before he could coax her back to the marriage bed.

This episode did no good at all for Tom's sex life, and it caused much local amusement. Needless to say, after this, he treated his second wife considerably better than his first.

Ben Volke and the Bewitched Cartwheel

Thomas Evans lived at Molleston Mountain, not far from Narberth. One evening he was returning home in his old-fashioned dog-cart from Haverfordwest Market. On the way he passed Deep Lake at the foot of Arnold's Hill. There he passed Ben Volke, who was also returning from Market, but on foot. Ben lived in a hovel near Canaston Bridge, and he was reputed to be a witch. "How be yer Tom?" said Ben. "Oh, middlin. How be yerself, Ben?" said Tom, as he passed by, giving his pony a whip. Ben was heavily laden, and had hoped for a lift. He scowled under his battered hat, but Tom was in a hurry and thought no more of it.

Soon Tom was far ahead and was starting up the hill. Looking behind him, he saw Old Ben in the distance, standing beneath a tall yew tree. A shiver ran up his spine as he thought that he could see other dark shapes moving in the dark November shadows. As he watched he saw Ben light his pipe, but instead of seeing the expected spark he saw flashes of lightning striking out in all directions. He felt the hair rising on the back of his neck, and cracked his whip in order to urge his pony onwards. Suddenly the

cart skidded to a halt, with the right wheel totally jamm-ed. Tom dismounted, but could find nothing which was obviously wrong. As soon as he stood beside the cart the wheel revolved quite freely. So he thought he had better walk alongside the horse and cart until he reached the top of the long hill. Then, feeling quite ex-hausted, he climbed back onto the cart and urged the pony onwards. Again the wheel jammed and the cart would not move.

...after that the wheel gave him no trouble whatsoever.

After this, Tom repeatedly climbed onto the cart and alighted, with the same result each time. Whenever he was seated snugly on board, the wheel would not move; whenever he walked alongside, the wheel moved quite freely. Now convinced that Ben had bewitched the wheel, Tom thought that there was nothing for it but to walk home alongside his cart, for a distance of six miles or more. He was not amused.

On the following Monday, Tom went to see Abe Biddle the magician, who lived in Millin Dingle. The great man consulted his book of mysteries, and confirmed that Ben Volke had bewitched the cartwheel. Then he told Tom how to break the spell. He had to take an iron nail and dip it into the blood of a toad. Then he had to drive it into a particular part of the wheel with a new iron hammer. The hammer had to have a handle of mountain ash. Tom followed the instructions exactly, and the spell was broken. After that the wheel gave him no trouble whatsoever.

The Curse of the Hayscastle Witch

Long ago there was a wild and violent young man who belonged to an ancient family in the eastern parts of Dewisland. He was immensely tall and sported a ferocious black beard. He had great strength and an uncontrollable temper, and he was greatly feared and disliked by all the local people. He was viewed very much as the black sheep of the family. He used to ride about the country lanes on a large horse, so heedless of other people's welfare that those who were in his way literally had to jump for their lives.

One evening while galloping madly along a lane on his way home from Haverfordwest, he knocked down and killed a little girl. Quickly her family and neighbours gathered round, and what with their cries and curses, and the oaths of the arrogant horseman, there was soon pandemonium. An old lady who lived in a nearby cottage heard all the commotion and came out to investigate. She had a reputation of being a witch (*gwrach or gwyddon*), and when she saw the dead child she told the bearded horseman that his soul was now in the hands of the evil one, and that when his time came to die Old Nick would send a huge black hound or *gwyllgi* to curse him and his descendants. The young man laughed at this, tossed a few coins to the bereaved family to cover their loss, and set off on his way. Soon afterwards his family, mindful of the fact that he could be charged with murder, sent him abroad and nothing was heard of him for many years.

But about 40 years later a middle-aged man of great strength and forceful personality came into Solva on one of the vessels that plied the coastal trade. The most striking thing about him was his thick hair and long black beard. He left his ship and went to live in a small cottage, and he obtained work as a labourer with Mr Raymond, a prosperous Solva merchant. He was still good-looking, and was clearly well educated; and in time he took a young wife who bore him several children. He gained a reputation for the shortness of his temper, and became involved in a number of fist fights. Gradually people started to recognize the physical and emotional traits of the ancient family in him, and some began to suspect that he was the "missing younger son" who had gone abroad from the Hayscastle area many years before. Finally he admitted to his origins during a night of revelry in a local tavern, and then stormed out, swearing that he would be more content to ride down all those present than drink with them. Then he slammed the door, and was gone into the night.

A fortnight later the man's young wife ran to the door of the local doctor in a state of shock. She pleaded with him to come to the cottage quickly; so he threw on his coat and followed her. When he came into the bedroom the man was on the bed with his limbs thrashing about horribly and with an awful expression of terror on his face. He kept shouting hysterically "Keep the dog away! Keep the dog away!" Nobody could control him or subdue him. This went on for some time, until at last his voice trailed away to a whisper, and he fell back dead. He was buried at Tregroes graveyard.

Succeeding generations of the deceased man's family were all haunted by the spectral hound; and the last head of the family to die, in 1923, was actually pursued by it one night in a lane near Hayscastle.

The Flying Witch of Marloes

There is not a single reference in the folk tale literature of Pembrokeshire to a witch actually flying through the air on a broomstick. For the most part their special powers are restricted to transformations into animals such as cats and hares, and placing curses on machines or individuals. However, a recent story from Marloes has proved the exception to the rule.

A local gentleman called David was making a telephone call from the village phone box one evening at about 9 pm. It was a

A witch making a spell from the inside of a magic circle. Note the surrounding imps and demons who are assisting her, and the two flying witches who are looking on.

dark evening, and the street lights were lit. Having finished his call, he was leaving the phone box when he saw, quite clearly, a witch on a broomstick flying across the road in front of him. She was about 10 ft above the road surface, and as David watched she swooped up towards the roof of a house next to the Two Foxes public house and simply appeared to pass into the roof. And so she disappeared from sight. David thinks thst she wore long garments that were dark in colour.

The observer was not particularly frightened by the encounter, but recalls that he was rather disappointed that the witch had not gone into his roof instead, where maybe he could later on have had an interesting chat with her.

Betty Foggy's Bothersome Spell

In the heyday of the Royal Naval Dockyard at Pembroke Dock the launch of each new ship was accompanied by celebration on a grand scale. Normally the reserved seats were in great demand, kept for local dignitaries, officers and their families. Those without Dockyard connections were seldom invited to the feasts.

In the year 1847 the time came to launch HMS *Lion*, the largest warship in the Royal Navy. This was a highly prestigious event, and competition for reserved seating was intense. When the great day arrived a strange old woman known as Betty Foggy came up to the Dockyard gate and asked to be given one of the reserved seats where she could listen to the speeches and see the breaking of the bottle on the ship's bows. But she was greeted with derision and told to go away. "In that case", she said, "there will be no launch today. You may all go home, good people." And off she went into the town.

The *Lion* was duly named, and the champagne broken on her bows. The dogshores were knocked away, but the vessel refused to budge. No matter what the Dockyard workers did to induce the vessel to move down the slipway, she remained firmly stuck. Eventually, to the embarrassment of the Dockyard officials, all the guests had to go off home. And the *Lion* remained immovable on the slipway until the next Spring tides came round, when she slid into the water without the slightest trouble.

The Phantom Witch of Cwmslade

Cwmslade was a small and very ancient cottage not far from Tufton, located on land which is now devoted to forestry. At the time of this story, during the Second World War, there was an American garrison at Puncheston, and over the mountain of Mynydd Castlebythe it was possible to see and hear the American army tanks firing at their targets.

Around 1943 an Englishman named Ron Stevens lived in the cottage and used it for training hawks; and in the holidays he was helped by Dick Harries, a twelve-year-old Welsh lad. One day the pair were feeding the hawks on raw meat in the little garden at the back of the cottage. Suddenly the lad noticed that the thick thorn hedge around the garden was moving. The hawks became alarmed, and as Ron Stevens and the boy tried to calm them down a black dog appeared to walk straight through the hedge, which was normally quite impenetrable. Ron told the boy to chase the dog away, and as he rose to do so a "big black woman" appeared straight in front of him.

The phantom witch (*gwyddon*) had a black hat on her head, and her white teeth curled right out over her bottom lip. Her clothes were all black, and her hands were encased as though in gloves and folded across her chest. She wore battered black boots, with the toes curled up. There was an ancient enigmatic smile on her face, and she walked slowly out of the garden, beckoning for Ron and the lad to follow. This they did, walking as if in a trance. Afterwards they noticed that they had been unable to talk at this time. The old woman led them through a gap in the thorn hedge towards a well, and there she disappeared.

Ron and the boy, still mesmerized, looked into the well, but the water was perfectly still. Nothing stirred. Then they were released from the spell. Not waiting to see what had happened to the phantom dog, the boy fled home, running straight across the bog whereas normally he skirted round it. When he arrived home he was totally exhausted and still in a state of shock. He collapsed on the passage floor in front of his mother, and for a fortnight afterwards he was too ill to get out of bed. Ron Stevens was so frightened by the episode that he moved out of the cottage the same evening, never to return. Not long afterwards the cottage was demolished to make way for forestry work, and the site is now lost in the dark shadows of the coniferous woodland.

The Strange Spell at Cwmslade

Two years after the events related above, when Dick left school, he went to work at Morfil, a big farm of the other side of the valley. At that time the farm was owned by a Mr Harries, no relation to Dick, who had moved into the area from England.

Early one morning, when Dick turned up for work, Mr Harries said to him "Good morning, Dick. Those wretched cattle have got out again. They are up in Cwmslade. I want you to go and fetch them back." "Yes yes," replied Dick. "I'll go and fetch them now." "Well," said the farmer. "There is no great hurry. You had better have your breakfast first and fetch them after." So Dick had his breakfast and then set off for Cwmslade. He could see the cattle near the old cottage in the cwm ahead of him. Before he reached the animals he came to the little stream which he had crossed many times before via a couple of convenient stepping stones. As he tried to jump onto the stones he suddenly became tight-chested and started gasping for breath. He tried again, but felt that something was smothering him. Every time he tried he lost his breath, and at last he thought to himself "I can't manage this. I'd better go back and tell the boss that there is something strange going on at the stream, so that I'm unable to fetch the cattle."

He turned to go back to the farm, but then felt rather foolish. Convinced that Mr Harries would not believe him, he returned to the stream and tried again to cross it. Again he was seized with panic, and struggled for breath. Furious that he could not cross such a tiny stream, with the cattle so close, he at last gave in and went back to the farm. When he explained to the farmer what had happened, Mr Harries said "Oh, don't be silly." "I'm sorry, but I just can't get over the stream!" said Dick. "What's wrong?" "When I try to jump onto the stones I lose my breath." "But that's absurd!" "I just can't do it." "Oh, very well! I'll come with you."

And so they both walked up to the stream where the cattle were. Watched by Mr Harries, the boy tried to jump across, but again became quite breathless. He stood rooted to the spot, gasping for air. So the farmer jumped across, without any trouble at all. Turning to Dick, he said "What's wrong with you? Come on -- jump!" The lad tried again, but again he lost his breath. Quite unable to understand what was affecting young Dick, Mr Harries collected the cattle and got them back across the stream. Then together the two of them drove the animals to the farm.

For years afterwards Dick tried to find some explanation for what had happened that morning in Cwmslade; but he could only conclude that he had been bewitched, or that there was some dark presence which refused to allow him to approach the cottage where, two years before, he had seen the Old Black Witch.

The Servant Girl of Gelli-fawr

The members of a well-known Gwaun Valley family were noted for their knowledge of witchcraft. It so happened that they applied to become members of Caersalem Chapel in Cilgwyn. However, one of their number could not resist casting a spell or *cyfaredd* on the very day that she was baptized. She bewitched a young servant girl of Gelli-fawr farm while sitting behind her in the chapel. The poor girl rushed out of her pew, and out of the chapel, and ran wildly about the roads of Cilgwyn. This continued for several days. Her father, having tried every means of pacifying her, went at last to Cwrt-y-Cadno in Carmarthenshire to consult Dr Harries, the well-known *dyn hysbys* or wise man.

Dr Harries asked no questions, but accurately told her father what had happened and even showed him the scene all over again in a mirror. He then gave him a piece of paper with some mysterious words written on it, which the girl had to wear on her breast. And this was quite sufficient to bring the poor girl back to normal again.

A Merry Dance for the Squire

Once upon a time there was an old lady called Nansi who lived in a rented cottage between Cardigan and Cilgerran. She had something of a reputation as a *gwrach* or witch, but she was friendly enough, and lived with her little grand-daughter Bethan.

Nearby there was a big mansion house, occupied by a squire who was well known in sporting circles as a huntsman. He owned the old lady's home, and many other cottages in the neighbourhood, but he charged high rents and made life difficult for his tenants. He was an arrogant man, not well liked in the community, and old Nansi found it hard to pay the rent with hardly any money coming in from week to week. One day he had a furious row with the old lady, and threatened to throw her and young Bethan out onto the street unless they kept up their rent payments. There was not much that Nansi could do, but one day she told her grand-daughter that she would teach the squire a lesson he would not forget in a hurry.

Not long after, old Nansi looked down towards the big house and saw that the squire was setting off towards the big fields with his dogs on a hare-coursing expedition. "Now then, Bethan bach," said Nansi, "we will give them a bit of a chase." And before the girl knew what was happening her grandmother had disappeared. She looked all over the cottage and then noticed a big hare near the front door. She opened the door, and the hare bounded off towards the fields. Then the squire saw the hare. He had one particularly fine black hound which was walking to heel, and he pointed at the hare with the command "Now, black dog!" Away sprang the hound towards the hare, and Bethan watched with horror as it came ever closer to its quarry.

Then Bethan shouted at the top of her voice "Now, grandma!", and watched with fascination as the hare took off across the field with the black hound in pursuit. Far into the distance they went, with the black dog after the hare, and the squire (who was somewhat overweight) puffing along after the dog. There was an almighty commotion, with the squire yelling and the other dogs barking. All the time Bethan saw that the hare kept just far enough ahead of the dog to keep the chase going, so that both the dog and the squire believed that it would soon be caught.

Through hedges and over ditches they went, with the dog getting more and more exhausted and the squire more and more muddy and covered with thorns and thistles as he slipped and fell over and over again. With a feeling of wonderment Bethan noticed that the hare did not seem to tire at all, rushing around with boundless energy across one field after another, and tempting and teasing both the dog and its master.

When this had gone on for a while various neighbours, attracted by all the noise, turned up to watch the performance, and soon their laughter echoed around the big fields and along the country lanes. With every twist and turn of the chase they cheered the hare on, while the squire became more and more furious with his predicament. At last he collapsed from sheer exhaustion, and so did his black dog. Watched by the ecstatic neighbours, the hare pranced around them a few times, as if to taunt them, and then loped off towards Nansi's cottage. On the way it passed Bethan, who had been standing on the hedge watching the entertainment from beginning to end. It hopped into the little garden, over the doorstep and in through the front door. Bethan ran inside after the hare, and when she got to the kitchen there was old Nansi again, sitting by the fire with a cheerful rosy glow on her face. Bethan said nothing, and neither did her grandmother, but they were both delighted.

The news of the squire's adventure with the cheeky hare travelled fast through the area, and there was loud laughter in the local inns as the tale was told and re-told many times over. The poor man was quite poorly for several weeks as a result of his exertions in the chase, and indeed as a result of the indignity he had suffered. He became the butt of many jokes among the poor tenants on his estate and also among the local gentry. His reputation as a great sportsman was damaged beyond repair.

But strange to relate, the squire became a better man as a result of the episode with the hare, and he never again treated his tenants with arrogance and disdain. He had a suspicion that the whole thing had something to do with old Nansi, although he could of course never prove it. Anyway, for the rest of her life the old lady was treated with courtesy and respect by her landlord, and life for young Bethan became a little more bearable as a result.

Bethan never forgot the events of that exciting day, and many years afterwards she told the story to a young man who wrote it down for future generations to enjoy.

The Bewitched Apples

Once upon a time (around the year 1810) there was an old witch who lived in Maenclochog. She was known at the time as a *gwraig hyspys*, and she was credited with many remarkable feats involving second sight, spells, and magic.

One hot day in the month of September a young man passed her garden and saw that her wonderful apple trees were laden down with ripe juicy apples. He was greatly tempted, and decided that nobody would miss a few apples since there was such a prolific crop. So he hopped over the hedge when nobody was looking, took off his shirt to turn it into a sort of makeshift bag, and filled it with apples. Then he hurried off home, quite sure that nobody had seen him.

Next day he fell mysteriously ill, and although his mother fed him plenty of ripe apples to make him better, he got worse and worse. The doctor could not decide what the cause of the illness was, nor could he give it a name. For several weeks the young man remained in bed, with his family becoming more and more worried. At last the young thief admitted to his mother that he had pinched the apples from the old lady down the road, and it immediately became clear to her that the old witch had placed the "evil eye" on her son.

Without further ado, the mother gathered up all the apples that were left, and took them in a bag back to the old witch. She apologized profusely for her son's wickedness, and as soon as the apples had been returned the young man was restored to perfect good health. After that, he stole no more apples from the old lady's garden, and neither did anybody else in the village, since news of such things as the mystery illness travels fast in a small community.

Magic Signs at Cresswell

Cresswell Quay is a beautiful spot at the inner end of the Cresswell River, one of the tidal creeks of the Milford Haven waterway. Not far from the Quay, on Cresswell Hill, there is a little valley called Cottage Dingle, in which there is a well. This well has been called Lady's Well since time immemorial, and it is associated in local legend with a number of ghostly figures who were referred to as "The White Ladies". We do not know how long ago these ghosts were in residence, but the locals were considerably frightened by them. Some time in the 1700s the mysterious spirits were banished from the vicinity by a local magician. He adopted the unusual technique of carving pentacles (five-pointed stars used as charms or occult symbols) into the bark of a number of beech trees alongside the road on Cresswell Hill. No doubt he also went through some form of exorcism at the same time. About a hundred years ago one of these pentacles could still be seen on the trunk of one of these beeches, about 15 feet above the ground. J Ceredig Davies, who visited Cresswell around 1900, reckoned that "the wound was evidently made well nigh a century ago, judging by its appearance."

Around 1890 a Pembrokeshire gentleman passed by a remote house in the vicinity of Cresswell which was occupied by an old Magician. He saw a number of pentacles cut into the bark of oak trees near the house, and asked the old man a few questions concerning the meaning of the strange signs. However, all he got in response was the following remark, short and to the point: "They be signs."

The Bewitched Cattle

Once upon a time there was a celebrated witch who lived near Mathry. She had something of a reputation for bewitching farm animals, and was known to cause trouble if she had a grudge against any of the local farmers. Local people also believed that she sometimes cast spells to order, for an appropriate fee.

One summers morning, bright and early, the servant-girl of a farm in the neighbourhood went down to the meadow to fetch the cows back to the farm for milking. When she got there she found all the cows sitting on their haunches like cats before a fire; and no matter how much she pushed them and shouted at them they refused to move. She went back to the farm and reported the problem to her master. He was involved in some dispute with the old witch, and immediately suspected that she had cast a spell. So he went off angrily to her cottage and told her off in no uncertain manner. Maybe he also came to some agreement over the dispute; but at any rate the old lady then followed him down to the meadow where the cows were still squatting. She told the farmer that there was nothing at all wrong with the cattle, and she went round the herd touching each animal lightly on the back. Immediately, the cows got back onto their feet and started to head for the cow-shed where they were to be milked.

Dealing with the Jordanston Witch

In the early Nineteenth Century there was a tradition in the Fishguard area that the only way of undoing the evil spell of a witch was to take out the heart of a bewitched animal and to burn it after filling it with iron objects such as pins and nails. On the completion of this gruesome business, it was further believed that the smoke from the burning heart would drift towards the witches house, regardless of the direction of the wind.

Around 1880 the Rev J.W. Evans was told by an old woman of Jordanston parish that when she was young there was an old witch who lived nearby. She was suspected of bewitching the cattle of a poor farmer who was a near neighbour. She caused so much trouble that in the end the people of the parish forced her to leave her cottage and to go and live elsewhere. However, no sooner had she left than the poor farmer's best cow died, and several of his suckling calves also became ill.

It was immediately realized that the angry and resentful old woman had placed a curse upon the farm. Someone who knew about witchcraft suggested that the only thing to do in the circumstances was to take the dead cow's heart and burn it in a big fire. This was done, and next day the old woman returned, as if drawn by some irresistible force, and healed the calves before going away again. After that, the poor farmer's animals were quite healthy.

She was suspected of bewitching the cattle of a poor farmer.

The Witch and the Baker's Wife

There was once an old witch in Fishguard who caused a great deal of trouble among the householders and shop-keepers. She would come knocking at people's doors and would ask for food and clothing, and said that she would cast a spell on anybody who refused to help her. So people used to do her bidding, afraid lest they offended her.

One of the shops regularly visited by the old witch was a bakery owned by Mr Rees. His wife eventually became fed up with all the calls on her charity, since times were not all that good for her own family, with children to feed and bills to be paid. So she determined to make a stand next time the old woman called, and asked among her friends about the most effective ways of finding protection against evil spells. She was advised to obtain a large iron nail from the blacksmith's shop, and this she did. Next time the old witch called, Mrs Rees opened the door, taking care to have the nail under her foot on the floor. She listened to the usual begging and threatening, but replied "Get away from my door! Now I'm not afraid of you, for I have my foot on a nail!"

In a great rage, the old witch shuffled off down the street, muttering to herself. But Mrs Rees kept her foot firmly on the nail until she went round the corner, and in doing so protected herself from the spells cast in her direction. After that, Mrs Rees was not bothered again by the old woman.

Witchcraft at Honey Harfat

During the Eighteenth Century there were witches in all the towns of Pembrokeshire, and some of them caused genuine fear in the hearts of townspeople. One such lived in the county town of Haverfordwest (Honey Harfat).

We do not know precisely where she lived, but she terrorized the town inhabitants, local farmers and peasantry for many years. She had the gift of second sight, and would inform neighbours (quite accurately) about events which would happen in their lives in the future. She had the ability to find lost objects, and helped in the recovery of many items which had been stolen. But her darker side predominated, and she seemed to rejoice in doing mischief and in casting spells on innocent victims. Those whom she disliked would be subjected to wicked pranks, causing "everything to go upside down with them". It was said that she could transform herself into a black cat, which would haunt the houses of her enemies.

There were rumours in the community that the old witch would consort with fellow witches on summer evenings in a dark wooded glen near the town, where strange dances and magic ceremonies took place. Some people even said that the old woman had sold her soul to "the prince of the air", and could therefore fly about in the sky on the proverbial broomstick..........

Mary of Llanstinan

The Squire of Llanstinan, not far from Trecwn, was a great sportsman who enjoyed hare coursing. But he was constantly frustrated by a certain hare, which used to lead his hounds a merry dance. The hare would always escape from them, leaving both he and his hounds quite exhausted. Day after day and mile after mile he and the dogs would follow the animal, but it would always disappear in the same general area above the deep wooded valley of Nant-y-Bugail. At last people began to suspect that the hare must really have been a witch having some fun at the squire's expense; and the gentleman was advised that he would only succeed in catching the hare if he went out with a horse and a dog of exactly the same colour.

So he went to great trouble to find a horse which matched the colour of his best dog, and next time he went out hunting he felt he was well prepared. Sure enough, the mysterious hare appeared in his big field, and off it went with the hounds and rider in hot pursuit. Now, for the first time, the hound and the horse managed to make up ground on the clever hare, and the squire became convinced that he would catch it at last. But then they came upon a remote cottage, and just before the dogs got to it the hare bolted through a little hole in the front door. The squire saw this as he came galloping up, so he dismounted and knocked on the door. It was opened by a rather breathless old woman who was well known to the squire. He said "Oh! It's just you, Mary!", and that was that. However, everybody in the neighbourhood became quite convinced that old Mary was indeed a witch. As for the mysterious hare, having had a bit of a shock, it was never seen again.

The Bewitching at Walton East

Around 1850 there was an old woman in Walton East who was supposed to be a witch (*gwyddon*). One day two young girls, daughters of a local farmer and his wife, were suddenly taken ill. It was widely assumed that the old woman had bewitched them, so the girls' mother went to her cottage and rebuked her with the words "Old woman! Why did you bewitch my daughters? Come and undo thy wickedness!"

The old woman denied that she had anything to do with the illness, but the mother would not believe her protestations and compelled her to come to the farmhouse. When they reached the front door of the house the old witch said "God bless thee." The girls were in bed in an upstairs room at the time, but only one of them heard the old women's words. She immediately recovered from her illness. However, the daughter who had not heard the release from the spell continued to be ill, and her condition even deteriorated. For fifteen years she refused to leave her bedroom and behaved very strangely. When anybody entered the room she hid under the bed-clothes like a rat, and she refused to eat her meals in the presence of anybody else.

At last the old woman died, and immediately the sick daughter started to recover. As the mortal remains of the witch decayed in the grave she became better and better, until she was completely well again. Eventually she married a wealthy local farmer. She lived a perfectly normal and fulfilling life in the Walton East area, and enjoyed the very best of health.

Witchcraft at Roch Castle

The tall tower of Roch Castle, perched on its volcanic crag, dominates the landscape around the north-eastern corner of St Bride's Bay. It marks the northernmost extent of Norman influence in this part of Pembrokeshire, and stands at the western end of the Landsker. The lordship which it controlled was remote and vulnerable to attack by the Welsh princes, and the castle was never built to its original design. Only the stone keep was completed and the lack of further progress on the building work may have been due to the sad and premature demise of the builder, Adam de la Roche.

Adam was the first feudal Norman lord of Roch in the twelfth century. One winters day he was cursed by a gwyddon or witch, who said that before a year would pass, he would die from the bite of an adder. Now adders were quite common in the dry places around the castle keep, and Adam became very fearful for his life.

Soon he was so affected by the witch's curse that he shut himself away in the topmost room of the tower, refusing to come down even in bad weather when it was most unlikely that he would encounter an adder. All his food and clothing and firewood had to be brought up to him as he lived the life of a recluse. As the seasons passed he began to relax a little, and after Christmas the tower was buffeted again by the storms of a typical Pembrokeshire winter.

With only one day to go until the end of the curse, Adam began to feel that he would survive. It was a bitterly cold evening, and as the light faded he ordered his old servant woman to bring up a new bundle of firewood from the store so that he could keep a good blaze going in his hearth overnight. This she did, and after stoking up the fire Adam settled down before its warmth and fell asleep.

But unknown to both the old woman and her master, an adder had chosen to hibernate in the bundles of firewood stowed outside, and had been carried up with the sticks into Adam's room. As the warmth spread around the room the adder woke from its hibernation. Later on Adam reached out to grab some more sticks for the fire......

And so it was that when the servants came up to their master's room next morning they found him dead, poisoned by the bite of an adder as the old witch had foretold.

Maggie of Pontfaen

Mr Griffiths of Maenclochog once related how his mother encountered a troublesome witch called Maggie when she was young. At the time (around 1820) his mother worked at the squire's house at Pontfaen, and whenever she went out in the morning to milk the cows she was greatly bothered by a hare. The animal pranced about and disturbed the cows, so that they became difficult to milk. She knew that the hare was really an old witch called Maggie who lived in the neighbourhood, and at last she complained to her master.

Next morning when she went out to milk the cows the squire came with her, and shot at the hare. Somehow the animal escaped, but the shot had wounded it and drawn blood. They watched it limping away into the undergrowth, leaving a trail of blood on the grass. Now the servant girl was happy, since a witch loses her power immediately on the drawing of blood. Sure enough, the girl was not bothered by the hare any more. Soon afterwards she decided to call on old Maggie, and she found her in bed, feeling not all well, with her leg all bandaged up.

Sally-Anne of Trefelyn

Sally-Anne was a shy, dark-haired girl who lived with her grandmother at Trefelyn, not far from Mathry. She was a lonely child, for the cottage where she lived was isolated in a deep valley, and there were few visitors because her grandmother was thought by the locals to be a witch or *gwyddon*.

Sally-Anne worked on a farm just outside the village of Mathry, and she walked there every morning at dawn. She had many farm duties, but she loved the animals so much that she quite neglected her work in the farmhouse on washing, cleaning, cooking and mending. The farmer's wife frequently had to hunt for her all over the farm, where she would invariably be found in the company of the sheep or cattle. She was reproached time and again, but when she did not mend her ways she was finally summoned to the farmer, who dismissed her and sent her on her way back to her grandmother. "And don't ever come back again!" he shouted angrily as tears welled up in her eyes.

"But the animals will fret terribly without me," she pleaded. "They need me to be with them." But the farmer remained unmoved, and the dejected child walked back across the fields to her cottage.

When she arrived and tearfully told her grandmother that she had lost her job the old woman was furious, for the small wages and rations of milk, butter and eggs were all they had to live on. For the rest of the day grandmother sat in her rocking-chair, stroking her black cat and muttering quietly to herself; and there she remained until far into the night.

Next morning, back on the farm, the farmer found the bull in a furious temper and the cows lowing and tugging at their chains and refusing to cooperate during milking. The cocks were fighting and the hens stopped laying. Many of the sheep and lambs broke out through the hedges and wandered off across fields belong to neighbouring farms. No matter what the farmer did, he could not control the animals, and by the evening he was getting seriously worried. "I have never seen anything like it," he said. "It is as if a strange spell has come over them."

That evening, at the little cottage called Trefelyn, Sally-Anne and her grandmother sat quietly in the candle-light. The girl was still very upset at the loss of her job but the old woman placed a hand on her shoulder. "Don't fret, child," she said. "As likely as not, you'll soon hear a knock on the door, and before the week is out you'll be back with your animals on the farm."

And so it was that next day the farmer arrived and begged Sally-Anne to come and work on the farm again.....

Hannah of Walton West

Once upon a time a farmer and his young daughter were travelling home by horse and cart towards Little Haven, having been to the fair at Haverfordwest. The little girl was fast asleep in the cart as it rattled along the rough road towards the setting sun. As they approached Walton West a gnarled old woman in a long black shawl appeared by the roadside. "Can you give a tired old woman a lift home?" she asked.

The farmer knew her as old Hannah, who was reported to be a witch (*gwyddon*). He nodded and invited her to climb up into the cart, for there is no point in tempting fate by being unkind to a witch. The cart rattled along for another mile or so, and suddenly the farmer's daughter awoke with a start to see the old lady wringing her hands and muttering to herself in a language she did not understand. At first she was frightened, because she too knew that Hannah was a witch; but the old lady looked quite kind and told the girl that she would never harm an innocent child.

At last the little girl plucked up enough courage to speak. "Do you cast magic spells?" she asked timidly. Hannah merely chuckled and continued to mumble to herself as the cart lurched along the rutted track. Then the girl spotted three teams of horses harrowing a field, under the control of three farm workers. She became mischievous, and asked the old lady if she could stop the three teams of horses with a magic spell. Old Hannah whispered some more strange words, and in an instant the first team of horses shied up as if confronted by a wall of flame. Then the second team shied up, causing the farm-boy to drop the reins and flee across the field. The third team carried on harrowing quite peacefully, just as if nothing at all had happened.

"Can you give a tired old woman a lift home?" she asked.

The girl watched expectantly, but Hannah appeared quite unconcerned. Then she turned to the girl and explained. "The third team cannot be affected by a magic spell," she said, "because the driver has a piece of mountain ash tied to his whip, and mountain ash has special properties." And so the cart continued to rattle and rumble its way towards Walton West.

Chapter Four--
Charming, Healing and Divination

Charms and Charming

As indicated in the Introduction, charms have been around in Pembrokeshire for a very long time, two of the most widespread being the pentacle symbol and the word "Abracadabra" written onto a piece of paper. Even today, it is quite common for people to carry charms or talismen around with them. Personal jewellery may incorporate locks of hair from your beloved, stones from special places, or little verses written out on small pieces of paper folded and contained within lockets or brooches. Astrological signs are widely used as charms on brooches, necklaces and bangles. Some of the holy wells of Pembrokeshire have scraps of clothing, shoes or other personal items fixed to them by individuals who are ill, or by their relatives. Coins are cast with reckless abandon into healing wells and springs in the hope of bringing "good luck", and the four-leaved clover is still thought of as a charm. Faith, superstition, ritual and fun are all involved in the process, but the main purpose of charms and charming is wish fulfillment.

In another strand to the charming weave, strange and supposedly efficacious medicines and pills were widely used before the advent of modern medicine, and there are many nineteenth-century records of "miraculous" cures which modern scientists find difficult to explain. There are many charming stories (in both senses of the word!) about ordinary people using charms in the county, and on the following pages we reproduce just a small selection of them. The important thing about these stories is that the users of the charms do not personally have any special skills or healing talents. In contrast, those who used charms and charming techniques in a "professional" way should be referred to as healers or charmers, and some stories about them are to be found on pages 88 to 91.

The Llanwnda Pills

Once upon a time a young lady who lived in Llanwnda was cleaning the windows of her cottage. It was a hot and humid day, with thunder in the air. The weather looked somewhat threatening, but as the black clouds piled up over Pencaer she carried on with her work, thinking that if a thunder-storm was to break she would get plenty of warning and would be able to retreat indoors in good time. However, with no warning whatsoever a mighty flash of lightning struck the nearby rocks of Garnwnda and there was a simultaneous crash of thunder, the like of which she had never heard before.

Quite literally, the poor girl was frightened out of her wits by this experience. She collapsed on the ground, and her family had to carry her indoors. She recovered somewhat, but from that day on she suffered from epileptic fits. Her family did not know what to do, and the family doctor could do little to help. At last a local dyn hysbys or magician was consulted, and he gave clear instructions as to what should be done. The girl's father agreed to do as the magician suggested, but the poor girl was told nothing. A few weeks later a local person died, and the parish grave-digger started to dig a grave in the old Llanwnda churchyard. The father went along to keep an eye on things, and sure enough, as the magician had predicted, some old human bones were uncovered in the grave and thrown out onto the pile of soil.

The poor girl was frightened out of her wits by this experience.

The father collected one of these bones, took it home and cleaned it carefully. Then, following the instructions he had been given, he ground it down into a fine powder which he made into pills. These pills, as specified in the charm, were given to the girl, who took them obediently. And from that day on she was cured of her epileptic fits.

The Horse Skull Treatment

Under the floors of many old Pembrokeshire cottages there are horse's skulls. When Mr Thomas of Jordanston was replacing the floor of his old house in 1901 he discovered no less than 20 skulls; he claimed that they were there to ensure good acoustics, and he carefully replaced them beneath the new floor. When the first Calvinistic Methodist Chapel was built in Caerfarchell, near St David's, in 1763, the acoustics were found to be quite unsatisfactory. When the congregation had suffered from 64 years of terrible echoes and reverberations, they decided to rebuild the chapel; and one William Lewis, a faithful chapel-goer who was a seaman by profession, was given the task of sorting out the noise problem. So when the new foundations were being put in William promised to provide two horse's skulls, which he guaranteed would sort out the trouble. For good measure he provided four skulls, and one was placed under each of the four corners of the building. Sure enough, when the new chapel was inaugurated, the congregation found that the "charmed" acoustics were magnificent.

    The Calvinistic Methodists were in principle fiercely opposed to all kinds of charms and superstitions, and it is interesting that they clearly considered the placing of the horse skulls under the foundations to be simply a matter of good building practice.

Llaethfaen, the Miraculous Stone

In the early 1800's there were a number of "quack doctors" who travelled through West Wales carrying with them healing stones. One such stone was referred to as "Llaethfaen". It was a small white pebble, slightly smaller than a hen's egg, and it was supposed to have miraculous properties. In particular, it was used as a preventative or cure for hydrophobia or rabies; if somebody had been bitten by a mad dog they would be given a milk mixture containing a small quantity of powder scraped off the stone, and this would guarantee that they would not be affected by rabies.

    Llaethfaen was kept at Gilfachwen, near Llandysul, and many hundreds of people were given the milk mixture over the years, especially during the summer months when rabid dogs had a tendency to go mad. In every case, so it was said, the treatment was successful.

Healers and Folk Medicine

In some parts of Pembrokeshire there are still men and women who have "special powers" just like the magicians or wise men of past centuries. Individuals often have a reputation and even a "calling" for healing, and some of the charmers and healers are reputed to have inherited strange skills from their parents. Some of them use modern techniques of healing through the use of herbs and other materials, re-awakening memories of methods which are thousands of years old. But others use techniques which appear to have no scientific rationale, involving lengths of wool, bits of straw, hand movements, and quotations from the Bible.

Gwen Davies and the Straw

In 1937 a woman called Gwen Davies was at work as a charmer in and around a South Pembrokeshire village, helping to heal the sick. One old man, who had been receiving medical attention for years but with no satisfactory result, was prevailed upon by his family to go and visit Gwen. This he did, and when he had explained the nature of his ailment and the treatment he had received, she sat him down in a chair with a table in front of it. She placed eleven pieces of straw on the table. Then she took a longer straw and waved it around the patient's head several times. Then she went to the table and moved one of the little pieces of straw. She repeated the "treatment" with the long straw, and then moved another of the short pieces to another part of the table. This went on for a long time, until all of the little pieces of straw had been moved from their original positions. Each time she went to the table, Gwen mumbled some words (they appeared to be Biblical quotations) in a low voice. Then, the treatment over, she announced: "You will get well now, but it will take time. Eat all you can get, but mind you don't touch no doctor's medicines, and definitely no hard drink." Gwen would take no payment. The patient left, did as instructed, and was completely cured.

Jones the Charmer of Martletwy

Mr Jones the Charmer of Martletwy was very much a local hero in the area around his home village. He had received the gift of charming from his mother as she lay on her deathbed. By the time he died in 1905 he had charmed over one hundred patients with excellent results, and he never took any payment for his work. According to local people, whenever he became involved in healing a cure was "absolutely certain".

Once upon a time a local minister had a seven year old son who fell into the living room fire while playing at home. The child was terribly burned about the head, and the family were convinced that he would die. The doctor was called, and he rushed to the vicarage. However, when he had examined the little boy he decided that there was nothing he could do to save him. Talk of the accident reached the ears of Mr Jones the Charmer, and immediately he made his way to the vicarage, for he and the vicar were old friends. The two men did not see eye to eye on everything, and the vicar often preached against charming, which was quite prevalent in the area at that time, referring to it as "the work of the Devil".

Jones the Charmer immediately made his way to the Vicarage.

When Mr Jones heard of the doctor's prognosis and when he saw the boy, he said "Let me charm the little boy. I know you don't believe in it, and that you have often preached against it, but never mind – if I don't cure him I will not have made matters worse. A drowning man will cling to a straw." The minister, with his mind wavering between despair and disbelief, at last agreed to his friend's request. So the Charmer went into the boy's bedroom where he lay in agony on his bed, with his head covered with appalling burns. This is what Mr Jones said: "Three little angels came from the East to try their virtue on fire and frost. In fire! Out frost! In the name of the Father and of the Son, and of the Holy Ghost." As he spoke he described a clockwise circle with the index finger of his right hand over the burnt area on the boy's head. This was done three times, with a repetition of the formula each time. Then he breathed three times on the affected part.

With that, Mr Jones took his leave and set off for home, saying that the boy would be much better by tomorrow. The vicar and his wife hardly dared to believe it, for they knew the child to be close to death. But true enough, by next day the boy was much brighter, and the burns were partly healed. Mr Jones returned and repeated the charm, and he repeated it again on the two following days. Then, as he set off he said "That will do the trick. Now the boy will be completely better in a fortnight's time."

And so it was. After two weeks the boy was out playing with his friends, with all traces of the burn gone. Never again did the vicar preach about charms as the work of the Devil.

The Wise Man of Templeton

About 25 years ago two cousins from the Haverfordwest area suffered from severe eczema on their forearms. This was a complaint that ran in the family. One of the cousins had a fine academic career and is still a well known teacher in the county. The other is a local farmer. For many years both men sought medical advice and tried various remedies in order to find a cure to their ailment. At long last the farmer was advised to consult the Wise Man of Templeton. We do not know the details, but the Wise Man used a secret charm, and in no time the eczema on the farmer's arm was healed.

The Wise Man said he could heal the teacher as well, if only he would come and pay him a visit. The farmer immediately rang up his cousin and advised him to go to Templeton to see the old healer. However, the teacher's education, and the scepticism that went with it, would not permit him to visit someone whom he considered to be a "quack doctor". To this day the farmer has had no recurrence of the eczema, whereas the academic continues to suffer from the affliction.

The Bleeding Charmer Jekky Arter

Jekky Arter of Williamston was a charmer who specialized in "stopping the blood". He was very well known all over Pembrokeshire. He had a magic wand which he would use only for certain cases. In the summer of 1839 a young man was pitching hay in a meadow adjoining the village of Cresselly. He was lifting up a very heavy "pick" of hay with his pitch-fork, but as he did so he burst a blood vessel and collapsed in a pool of blood. Normally he would have died in a few minutes, but Jekky happened to be nearby. The other farm labourers shouted to him in a frenzy and he rushed over to see what the commotion was all about.

On finding the young man on the ground Jekky immediately set to work. He dipped his finger in the young man's blood and signed him with a cross on his forehead. As he did this he muttered the following words from Ezekiel, Chapter 16, Verse 6: "And when I passed by thee, and saw thee polluted in thine own blood, I said unto thee when thou wast in thy blood, Live. Yea, I said unto thee when thou wast in thy blood, Live." He then stretched out his hand over the patient, as if in the act of blessing him. This process was repeated over and again until he had made the incantation nine times. The bleeding stopped immediately, and the young man was taken away to rest and recover. The case caused a sensation in the Cresselly area, and was long remembered in the neighbourhood as a remarkable demonstration of Jekky's powers. When Jekky died around 1845 his skill died with him, and his magic wand was lost.

Divination and Prophecy

The Ram's Shoulder-blade

The Flemings who settled in the Haverfordwest area in the Twelfth Century were renowned for their powers of divination. They used for this purpose the right shoulder-blades of rams which had been boiled (not roasted) and stripped of all flesh.

One William Mangunel was well known for his special powers, as was his young wife. But his wife was unfaithful, and William knew that the child she was carrying was not his but that of his own grandson. He was sorely troubled by this incestuous relationship, and determined to gain an admission from his wife as to her wicked ways. One day he took a ram from his flock, and killed it. Two days later, pretending that it was gift from a neighbour, he presented the carcass to his wife and suggested that it should be prepared for supper that very same evening. She sent it down to the cook to be prepared, and in due course they sat down at the dinner table and were served with fine portions of steaming mutton and fresh vegetables.

Before they started to eat the meat, William nonchalantly passed his wife the right shoulder-blade of the animal, boiled according to the recipe and now carefully cleaned. She took the bone and examined it minutely, fingering the cracks and all its secret markings. Her study of the prophetic bone continued for some little time, and then with a smile she threw it onto the table. William appeared unconcerned, but pressed her as to the cause of her amusement. Without thinking about what she was saying, she laughed "Husband, the man from whose flock this ram was taken has a wife who has broken the marriage vows. What is more," she continued, "at this very moment she is pregnant from commerce with his grandson."

Too late she realized that the ram had not come from a neighbour's flock but from their own, and that she had been trapped by her husband into a confession. William was not angry but downcast, for, as he said, it was he who had to face the public humiliation. As for the unfaithful wife, she was covered with confusion and then overcome with remorse. Sadly, we do not know what happened to her baby, or whether she really mended her wicked ways.

Rhamanta in Pembrokeshire

The custom of "rhamanta" or romantic divination, by which young people of marrying age seek to discover who their future husbands or wives might be, was widespread in Pembrokeshire well into the twentieth century. During the 1800's there was one trick which was supposed to be particularly effective. This was called the "Maid's Trick", and it could only be used by a virgin. If anybody tried it who was not a virgin, there was likely to be serious trouble with the fairies.

On Christmas Eve, or on one of the three "Spirit Nights" (*Teir-nos Ysprydion* in Welsh), the inquisitive young lady would creep downstairs after the old folk were fast asleep. Then she would put a good pile of coal or logs on the fire, lay a clean cloth on the table, and lay out as fine a feast of food and drink as she could find in the larder. For some reason, a hot toasted cheese sandwich was supposed to be particularly efficacious for this trick. Then, with the feast prep-ared and the fire blazing merrily, the girl would take off her clothes, piece by piece, while standing before the fire. Finally she would stand naked on the hearth, no doubt wishing that her future husband would somehow see her in his dreams. Her last and closest item of clothing would then be washed in a pail of clear spring water on the hearth, and would be spread to dry on a chair-back turned towards the fire. Finally she would go to bed, listening intently for her future husband, whose apparition was confidently expected to come to eat the prepared feast. On the arrival of the beloved spirit, the young lady was allowed to peep through the keyhole or through a crack in the bedroom door so as to identify the feasting guest.

.....*finally she would go to bed, listening intently for her future husband.*

It was claimed that this piece of divination worked well, and that many Pembrokeshire lasses had glimpsed their current lovers (or even some unexpected apparition) after performing the correct ceremonial. Further, it was guaranteed that after the appearance of the apparition, a happy marriage would occur within twelve months. But not all those who used the trick were pleased, and it was said in Pembrokeshire that on more than one occasion the expectant young lady, after going through all the motions of the ceremony, was horrified to see through the bedroom keyhole a terrible black-furred monster with fiery eyes and a long tail, gorging itself on the prepared feast with its whiskers dripping gravy. Naturally, young ladies who saw such a sight were doomed to a life of spinsterhood.......

The Missing Falcon's Eggs

During the 1980's, Pembrokeshire's few remaining pairs of peregrine falcons were struggling for survival. There were many thefts of eggs from falcon nests on the cliffs, and members of the local Wildlife Trust and the RSPB kept a constant watch on the most vulnerable nest sites during the nesting season in order to frighten off would-be nest robbers.

One such nest on the north coast was being watched night and day by Trust members. One member left for home at the end of his shift, having ascertained that the eggs in the nest were safe. But when his colleague arrived after a little while the eggs had gone. Clearly somebody must have had not only the nest but also the nest-watchers under surveillance. He had got at the eggs as soon as the way was clear, and had made his escape, probably aided by at least one accomplice.

The alarm was immediately raised, and the police were informed of the egg theft. They swung into action at once, and soon there were road blocks throughout the area, while Trust members scoured the fields, footpaths and lanes near the nest site. But there was no sign anywhere of the criminals.

At last somebody had a bright idea. There was, apparently, a meeting of diviners going on at that very moment in St Dogmaels, and it was thought that they might be able to help. So they were enlisted to the cause, and willingly agreed to see what they could do. They got out their maps and pendulums, and put their heads together. At last a message came to the police. The diviners had seen a sign, and they suggested that a red Fiat car travelling on the A40 towards St Clears with two passengers should be stopped and searched. Accordingly a road block was set up, and sure enough, along came a red Fiat with two men inside. They were acting very suspiciously, and were most reluctant to open the boot of their car when asked to do so by the police officers.

At last the men opened the boot of the car – to reveal net, lamp, gaff and two gleaming salmon freshly poached from the River Teifi. The men were duly arrested and charged, but the missing falcon eggs were never found.

Later, the St Dogmaels diviners apologized to the police for their lack of precision – they had all agreed that there was "something fishy" about the red Fiat, but they had, from a distance of 30 miles or so, been unable to discern exactly what the boot of the car contained!

Meilyr the Indelicate Prophet

One of the strangest stories given in the writings of Giraldus concerns a man called Meilyr, who hailed originally from the city of Caerleon. He was a soothsayer who was reputed to be able to explain the occult and foretell the future. When he was a young man he was very much in love with a young lady who lived near the city. One Palm Sunday he met his beloved out in the country in a peaceful and beautiful spot, and it seemed to both of them too good an opportunity to be missed. Meilyr was enjoying himself in her arms and "tasting her delights" when suddenly instead of the beautiful girl he found in his embrace a horrible hairy creature with long rough hair and a face too terrible to look upon. The experience was so profound that his wits deserted him and he became, in an instant, quite mad. He remained in this condition for many years, and eventually he was sent to the Monastery of St David's in the hope that he might there recover his sanity.

The saintly monks of St David's nursed him back to health, and at last he was able to resume his place in the community. But for the rest of his life he retained a close familiarity with unclean spirits. He was able to see them, recognise them, and call them each by his own name. According to the people he would talk to them as if they were close friends, and they would assist him in solving problems and in foretelling the future. Some said that he knew far too much for his own good. He was particularly adept at foretelling events in the near neighbourhood, and many people sought his assistance if they had been victims of some crime.

In his dealings with familiar spirits, Meilyr would often describe them as appearing in the form of huntsmen with horns hanging around their necks. Apparently he did not have many dealings with animal spirits, unlike some of the other soothsayers. If someone should tell a lie in his presence, Meilyr would immediately be aware of it, for he would see a demon dancing on the liar's tongue. If he looked at a book which contained some false statement, or which aimed to deceive the reader, he could immediately put his finger on the offending passage. When asked how he could do this, he would say that a demon was pointing out the falsehood for him. When he visited the dormitory of the Monastery at St David's he would point to the bed of any monk who harboured wicked thoughts, and he would denounce those who were afflicted by the vices of lust, gluttony, and greed.

Giraldus described a number of incidents by which Meilyr had caused severe embarrassment to those around him. On one occasion he revealed in confidence to Cynan, the good and saintly Abbot of Whitland, that he had received a vision of a local woman, and asked the Abbot whether he had anything to do with her. At this the holy man wept, and confessed to Meilyr that he had lusted after her. The Abbot allowed himself to be whipped by three of his monks, this being the punishment for his terrible sin.

On another occasion Meilyr predicted the downfall of Enoch the Abbot of Strata Marcella. He said that the Abbot would be ruined, for on that very day he would run off with a nun, thereby causing great scandal within the ecclesiastical community. Strata Marcella was a long way away, but people noted the date on which Meilyr had made his prophecy; and sure enough, eight days later news came through from distant parts that the Abbot had indeed run off with a nun, and was in disgrace. When Meilyr was asked how it was that he could be aware of such an event more than 100 miles away, he simply said that he had learned of it from a demon in the guise of a huntsman who had visited him early in the morning. Interestingly enough, in this case also the sinner came to repent. Enoch returned to his monastery a humble and chastened man, and according to the brothers in the Monastery he became stronger and more saintly following his experience.

Meilyr continued to embarrass the great and the good with his prophecies and insights for the rest of his life. In the year 1174, having left the sanctuary of St David's, he was in Usk Castle. He prophesied that some weeks later the castle would be attacked by the Earl of Clare, and that he himself would be wounded in military action. He said that the castle would fall to the enemy, but that he would escape from Usk alive. And so it came to pass. Meilyr was very badly injured in the battle. He escaped, but died soon afterwards from his wounds.

Commenting on Meilyr's sad end, Giraldus was clearly uncertain whether to treat the soothsayer as a friend or enemy of God. On balance he seems to have considered Meilyr to have been on the side of the devil, and his epitaph was as follows: "The Enemy knows how to favour his friends, but this is how he rewards them in the end".